HEALTH CARE ISSUES, COSTS AND ACCESS

THE HEALTH CARE FRAUD AND ABUSE PROGRAM

HEALTH CARE ISSUES, COSTS AND ACCESS

Additional books in this series can be found on Nova's website under the Series tab.

Additional E-books in this series can be found on Nova's website under the E-book tab.

HEALTH CARE ISSUES, COSTS AND ACCESS

THE HEALTH CARE FRAUD AND ABUSE PROGRAM

LORENA TOWNSEND
EDITOR

nova publishers
New York

For permission to use material from this book please contact us:
Telephone 631-231-7269; Fax 631-231-8175
Web Site: http://www.novapublishers.com

Additional color graphics may be available in the e-book version of this book.

Library of Congress Cataloging-in-Publication Data

ISBN: 978-1-62417-425-4

Published by Nova Science Publishers, Inc. ✝ New York

CONTENTS

Preface		**vii**
Chapter 1	Health Care Fraud and Abuse Control Program Annual Report for Fiscal Year 2011 *The Department of Health and Human Services and The Department of Justice*	**1**
Chapter 2	Health Care Fraud and Abuse Control Program: Improvements Needed in Controls Over Reporting Deposits and Expenditures *United States Government Accountability Office*	**117**
Index		**151**

PREFACE

This book provides an overview of The Health Insurance Portability and Accountability Act of 1996 (HIPAA) which established a national Health Care Fraud and Abuse Control Program (HCFAC) under the joint direction of the Attorney General and the Secretary of the Department of Health and Human Services (HHS), acting through the Inspector General, and designed to coordinate Federal, state and local law enforcement activities with respect to health care fraud and abuse. In its fifteenth year of operation, the HCFAC's continued success again confirms the soundness of a collaborative approach to identify and prosecute the most egregious instances of health care fraud, to prevent future fraud or abuse, and to protect program beneficiaries.

Chapter 1 – The Health Insurance Portability and Accountability Act of 1996 (HIPAA) established a national Health Care Fraud and Abuse Control Program (HCFAC or the Program) under the joint direction of the Attorney General and the Secretary of the Department of Health and Human Services (HHS), acting through the Inspector General, designed to coordinate Federal, state and local law enforcement activities with respect to health care fraud and abuse. In its fifteenth year of operation, the Program's continued success again confirms the soundness of a collaborative approach to identify and prosecute the most egregious instances of health care fraud, to prevent future fraud or abuse, and to protect program beneficiaries.

Chapter 2 – To help combat fraud and abuse in health care programs, including Medicare and Medicaid, Congress enacted the Health Care Fraud and Abuse Control (HCFAC) program as part of the Health Insurance Portability and Accountability Act of 1996 (HIPAA).

HIPAA requires that the Departments of Health and Human Services (HHS) and Justice (DOJ) issue a joint annual report to Congress on amounts deposited to and appropriated from the Federal Hospital Insurance (HI) Trust Fund for the HCFAC program.

In April 2005, GAO reported on the results of its review of HCFAC program activities for fiscal years 2002 and 2003 and made recommendations to HHS and DOJ.

The objectives of this requested review were to assess the extent to which HHS and DOJ (1) took actions to address the recommendations made in the 2005 report and (2) designed effective controls over reporting HCFAC deposits and expenditures for fiscal years 2008 and 2009. GAO reviewed HHS and DOJ documentation; selected nongeneralizable samples; and interviewed agency officials.

In: The Health Care Fraud and Abuse Program
Editor: Lorena Townsend
ISBN: 978-1-62417-425-4

Chapter 1

HEALTH CARE FRAUD AND ABUSE CONTROL PROGRAM ANNUAL REPORT FOR FISCAL YEAR 2011*

The Department of Health and Human Services and The Department of Justice

General Note
All years are fiscal years unless otherwise noted in the text.

EXECUTIVE SUMMARY

The Health Insurance Portability and Accountability Act of 1996 (HIPAA) established a national Health Care Fraud and Abuse Control Program (HCFAC or the Program) under the joint direction of the Attorney General and the Secretary of the Department of Health and Human Services (HHS)[1], acting through the Inspector General, designed to coordinate Federal, state and local law enforcement activities with respect to health care fraud and abuse. In its fifteenth year of operation, the Program's continued success again confirms the soundness of a collaborative approach to identify and prosecute

* This is an edited, reformatted and augmented version of The Department of Health and Human Services and The Department of Justice, dated February 2012.

the most egregious instances of health care fraud, to prevent future fraud or abuse, and to protect program beneficiaries.

Monetary Results

During Fiscal Year (FY) 2011, the Federal government won or negotiated approximately $2.4 billion in health care fraud judgments and settlements[2], and it attained additional administrative impositions in health care fraud cases and proceedings. As a result of these efforts, as well as those of preceding years, in FY 2011, approximately $4.1 billion was deposited with the Department of the Treasury and the Centers for Medicare & Medicaid Services (CMS), transferred to other Federal agencies administering health care programs, or paid to private persons during the fiscal year. Of this $4.1 billion, the Medicare Trust Funds[3] received transfers of approximately $2.5 billion during this period, and over $599.9 million in Federal Medicaid money was similarly transferred separately to the Treasury as a result of these efforts. The HCFAC account has returned over $20.6 billion to the Medicare Trust Funds since the inception of the Program in 1997.

Enforcement Actions

In FY 2011, the Department of Justice (DOJ) opened 1,110 new criminal health care fraud investigations involving 2,561 potential defendants. Federal prosecutors had 1,873 health care fraud criminal investigations pending, involving 3,118 potential defendants, and filed criminal charges in 489 cases involving 1,430 defendants. A total of 743 defendants were convicted of health care fraud-related crimes during the year. Also in FY 2011, DOJ opened 977 new civil health care fraud investigations and had 1,069 civil health care fraud matters pending at the end of the fiscal year. In FY 2011, Federal Bureau of Investigation (FBI) heath care fraud investigations resulted in the operational disruption of 238 criminal fraud organizations, and the dismantlement of the criminal hierarchy of more than 67 criminal enterprises engaged in health care fraud. In FY 2011, HHS' Office of Inspector General (HHS/OIG) excluded 2,662 individuals and entities. Among these were exclusions based on criminal convictions for crimes related to Medicare and Medicaid (1,015); or to other health care programs (233); for patient abuse or neglect (206); or as a result of licensure revocations (897). In addition,

HHS/OIG imposed civil monetary penalties against, among others, providers and suppliers who knowingly submitted false claims to the Federal government. HHS/OIG also issued numerous audits and evaluations with recommendations that, when implemented, would correct program vulnerabilities and save program funds.

INTRODUCTION

ANNUAL REPORT OF THE ATTORNEY GENERAL AND THE SECRETARY DETAILING EXPENDITURES AND REVENUES UNDER THE HEALTH CARE FRAUD AND ABUSE CONTROL PROGRAM FOR FISCAL YEAR 2011

As Required by Section 1817(k)(5) of the Social Security Act

Statutory Background

The Social Security Act Section 1128C(a), as established by the Health Insurance Portability and Accountability Act of 1996 (P.L. 104-191, HIPAA or the Act), created the Health Care Fraud and Abuse Control Program, a far-reaching program to combat fraud and abuse in health care, including both public and private health plans. As was the case before HIPAA, amounts paid to Medicare in restitution or for compensatory damages must be deposited in the Medicare Trust Funds. The Act requires that an amount equaling recoveries from health care investigations – including criminal fines, forfeitures, civil settlements and judgments, and administrative penalties – also be deposited in the Trust Funds. All funds deposited in the Trust Funds as a result of the Act are available for the operations of the Trust Funds. The Act appropriates monies from the Medicare Hospital Insurance Trust Fund to an expenditure account, called the Health Care Fraud and Abuse Control Account (the Account), in amounts that the Secretary and Attorney General jointly certify as necessary to finance anti-fraud activities. The maximum amounts available for certification are specified in the Act. Certain of these sums are to be used only for activities of the HHS/OIG, with respect to the Medicare and Medicaid programs. In FY 2006, the Tax Relief and Health Care Act (TRHCA) (P.L 109-432, §303) amended the Act so that funds allotted from the Account are "available until expended." TRHCA also allowed for yearly increases to the Account based on the change in the consumer price index for all urban consumers (all items; United States city average) (CPI-U) over the previous fiscal year for fiscal years for 2007 through 2010.[2] In FY 2010, the Patient Protection and Affordable Care Act, as amended by the Health Care and Education Reconciliation Act, collectively referred to as the Affordable Care Act (P.L. 111-148, ACA) extended permanently the yearly increases to the Account based upon the change in the consumer price index for all urban consumers or CPI-U. In FY 2011, the Secretary and the Attorney General certified $297.7 million in mandatory funding for appropriation to the Account. Additionally, Congress appropriated $310.4 million in discretionary funding. A detailed breakdown of the allocation of these funds is set forth later in this report. HCFAC appropriations generally supplement the direct appropriations of HHS and DOJ that are devoted to health care fraud enforcement and funded approximately three-fourths of HHS/OIG's appropriated budget in FY 2011. (Separately, the FBI received $128.4 million from HIPAA which is discussed in the Appendix.) Under the joint direction of the Attorney General and the Secretary, the Program's goals are:

1. to coordinate Federal, state and local law enforcement efforts relating to health care fraud and abuse with respect to health plans;
2. to conduct investigations, audits, inspections, and evaluations relating to the delivery of and payment for health care in the United States;
3. to facilitate enforcement of all applicable remedies for such fraud;
4. to provide guidance to the health care industry regarding fraudulent practices; and
5. to establish a national data bank to receive and report final adverse actions against health care providers and suppliers.

The Act requires the Attorney General and the Secretary to submit a joint annual report to the Congress which identifies both:

1. the amounts appropriated to the Trust Funds for the previous fiscal year under various categories and the source of such amounts; and
2. the amounts appropriated from the Trust Funds for such year for use by the Attorney General and the Secretary and the justification for the expenditure of such amounts.

Additionally, this report addresses language in the annual discretionary HCFAC appropriation (Public Law 111-117, made applicable in FY 2011 by Public Law 112-10, "DOD and Full-Year Continuing Appropriations Act of 2011") requiring that this report "include measures of the operational efficiency and impact on fraud, waste, and abuse in the Medicare, Medicaid, and CHIP programs for the funds provided by this appropriation."

This annual report fulfills the above statutory requirements.

MONETARY RESULTS

As required by the Act, HHS and DOJ must detail in this Annual Report the amounts deposited to the Medicare Trust Funds, and the source of such deposits. In FY 2011, approximately $4.1 billion was deposited with the Department of the Treasury and the Centers for Medicare & Medicaid Services (CMS), transferred to other Federal agencies administering health care programs, or paid to private persons during the fiscal year. The following chart provides a breakdown of the transfers/deposits:

Total Transfers/Deposits by Recipient FY 2011	
Department of the Treasury	
Deposits to the Medicare Trust Funds, as required by HIPAA	
Gifts and Bequests	$5,399
Amount Equal to Criminal Fines	$1,195,736,438
Civil Monetary Penalties	$16,495,458
Asset Forfeiture	$22,401,515
Penalties and Multiple Damages	$578,413,099
Subtotal	$1,813,051,909
Centers for Medicare & Medicaid Services	
HHS/OIG Audit Disallowances – Recovered - Medicare	$74,057,438
Restitution/Compensatory Damages	$660,522,078
Subtotal*	$734,579,516
Grand Total of Amounts Transferred to the Medicare Trust Funds	$2,547,631,425
Restitution/Compensatory Damages to Federal Agencies	
TRICARE	$74,423,629
Veteran's Administration	$20,238,404
HHS/OIG Cost of Audits, Investigations and Compliance Monitoring	$8,949,927
Office of Personnel Management	$53,035,272
Other Agencies	$11,276,161
Federal Share of Medicaid	$599,911,275

(Continued)

Total Transfers/Deposits by Recipient FY 2011	
HHS/OIG Audit Disallowances – Recovered - Medicaid	$354,092,195
Subtotal	$1,121,926,863
Relators' Payments**	$419,484,976
TOTAL ***	$4,089,043,264

* Restitution, compensatory damages, and recovered audit disallowances include returns to both the Medicare Hospital Insurance (Part A) Trust Fund and the Supplemental Medical Insurance (Part B) Trust Fund.

**These are funds awarded to private persons who file suits on behalf of the Federal government under the *qui tam* provisions of the False Claims Act, 31 U.S.C. § 3730(b).

***State funds are also collected on behalf of state Medicaid programs; only the Federal share of Medicaid funds transferred to CMS are represented here.

The above transfers include certain collections, or amounts equal to certain collections, required by HIPAA to be deposited directly into the Medicare Trust Funds. These amounts include:

1. Gifts and bequests made unconditionally to the Trust Funds, for the benefit of the Account or any activity financed through the Account;
2. Criminal fines recovered in cases involving a federal health care offense, including collections under section 24(a) of Title 18, United States Code (relating to health care fraud);
3. Civil monetary penalties in cases involving a federal health care offense;
4. Amounts resulting from the forfeiture of property by reason of a federal health care offense, including collections under section 982(a)(7) of Title 18, United States Code; and
5. Penalties and damages obtained and otherwise creditable to miscellaneous receipts of the general fund of the Treasury obtained under sections 3729 through 3733 of Title 31, United States Code (known as the False Claims Act, or FCA), in cases involving claims related to the provision of health care items and services (other than funds awarded to a relator, for restitution or otherwise authorized by law).

PROGRAM ACCOMPLISHMENTS

Expenditures

In the fifteenth year of operation, the Secretary and the Attorney General certified $297.7 million in mandatory funding as necessary for the Program. Additionally, Congress appropriated $310.4 million in discretionary funding. The following chart gives the allocation by recipient:

FY 2011 ALLOCATION OF HCFAC APPROPRIATION			
Organization	Mandatory Allocation[5]	Discretionary Allocation	Total Allocation
Department of Health and Human Services			
Office of Inspector General[6]	197,998,020	29,730,420	227,728,440
Office of the General Counsel	8,887,870	0	8,887,870
Administration on Aging	3,312,080	0	3,312,080
Food and Drug Administration	3,377,220	0	3,377,220
Centers for Medicare & Medicaid Services	22,292,322	250,917,160	273,209,482
Subtotal	235,867,512	280,647,580	516,515,092
Department of Justice			
United States Attorneys	31,400,000	9,770,759	41,170,759
Civil Division	18,972,139	2,396,624	21,368,763
Criminal Division	1,580,000	4,258,579	5,838,579
Civil Rights Division	3,432,688	2,091,312	5,524,000
Nursing Home and Elder Justice Initiative	1,000,000	0	1,000,000
Federal Bureau of Investigation[7]	0	3,946,994	3,946,994
Justice Management Division	200,000	0	200,000
Department of Justice - Other	5,235,606	7,266,152	12,501,758
Subtotal	61,820,433	29,730,420	91,550,853
TOTAL[8]	297,687,945	310,378,000	608,065,945

Accomplishments

Overall Recoveries

During this fiscal year, the Federal government won or negotiated approximately $2.4 billion in judgments and settlements, and it attained additional administrative impositions in health care fraud cases and proceedings. The Medicare Trust Funds received transfers of approximately $2.5 billion during this period as a result of these efforts, as well as those of preceding years; and another $599.9 million in Federal Medicaid money was transferred to the Treasury separately as a result of these efforts. 9

In addition to these enforcement actions, numerous audits, evaluations and other coordinated efforts yielded recoveries of overpaid funds, and prompted changes in federal health care programs that reduce vulnerability to fraud.[10]

The return-on-investment (ROI) for the HCFAC program, since 1997, is $5.1 returned to every $1.0 expended. The 3-year average (2009-2011) ROI is $7.2 to $1.0, which is $2.1 higher than the historical average. Due to the fact that the annual ROI can vary from year to year depending on the number of cases that are settled or adjudicated during that year, DOJ and HHS use a three-year rolling average ROI for results contained in the report. Additional information on how the ROI is calculated can be found in the Appendix.

Departmental Collaboration

Health Care Fraud Prevention & Enforcement Action Team (HEAT)

The Attorney General and the HHS Secretary maintain regular consultation at both senior and staff levels to facilitate, coordinate and accomplish the goals of the HCFAC Program. On May 20, 2009, Attorney General Holder and Secretary Sebelius announced the Health Care Fraud Prevention & Enforcement Action Team (HEAT), a new effort with increased tools and resources, and a sustained focus by senior level leadership to enhance collaboration between the Departments of Health and Human Services and Justice. With the creation of the new HEAT effort, DOJ and HHS pledged a cabinet-level commitment to prevent and prosecute health care fraud. HEAT, which is jointly led by the Deputy Attorney General and HHS Deputy Secretary, is comprised of top level law enforcement agents, prosecutors, attorneys, auditors, evaluators, and other staff from DOJ and HHS and their operating divisions, and is dedicated to joint efforts across government to both prevent fraud and enforce current anti-fraud laws around the country. The Medicare Fraud Strike Force teams are a key component of HEAT.

The mission of HEAT is:

- To marshal significant resources across government to prevent waste, fraud and abuse in the Medicare and Medicaid programs and crack down on the fraud perpetrators who are abusing the system and costing us all billions of dollars.

- To reduce skyrocketing health care costs and improve the quality of care by ridding the system of perpetrators who are preying on Medicare and Medicaid beneficiaries.
- To highlight best practices by providers and public sector employees who are dedicated to ending waste, fraud, and abuse in Medicare.
- To build upon existing partnerships between DOJ and HHS, such as our Medicare Fraud Strike Force Teams, to reduce fraud and recover taxpayer dollars.

Since its creation in May 2009, HEAT has focused on key areas for coordination and improvement. HEAT members are working to identify new enforcement initiatives and areas for increased oversight and prevention to increase efficiency in pharmaceutical and device investigations. DOJ and HHS have expanded data sharing and improved information sharing procedures in order to get critical data and information into the hands of law enforcement to track patterns of fraud and abuse, and increase efficiency in investigating and prosecuting complex health care fraud cases. The departments established a cross-government health care fraud data intelligence sharing workgroup to share fraud trends, new initiatives, ideas, and success stories to improve awareness across the government of issues relating to health care fraud.

Both departments also have increased training to prevent honest mistakes and help stop potential fraud before it happens. This includes CMS compliance training for providers, HHS/OIG's HEAT Provider Compliance Training series, ongoing meetings at U.S. Attorneys' Offices (USAOs) with the public and private sector, and increased efforts by HHS to educate specific groups – including elderly and immigrant communities – to help protect them. DOJ launched a new Medicare Fraud Strike Force training program designed to teach the Strike Force concept and case model to prosecutors, law enforcement agents, and administrative support teams, with involvement from both DOJ and HHS. CMS and HHS/OIG are providing ongoing training to DOJ and HHS staff on the use of new technology to catch and quickly turn off funding to those who are defrauding the system.

To achieve the mission and objectives of HEAT, the Attorney General and HHS Secretary promoted several HEAT initiatives during the fiscal year:

- Expanded the Medicare Fraud Strike Force to Chicago, IL, and Dallas, TX, which brought the total number of cities with Strike Force teams to nine.
- In the largest-ever federal health care fraud takedown, measured by number of defendants, Strike Force prosecution teams charged 115 defendants in nine cities, including doctors, nurses, health care company owners and executives, and others, for their alleged participation in Medicare fraud schemes involving more than $240 million in false billing.
- In the largest-ever federal health care fraud takedown, measured by fraudulent billings, Strike Force prosecution teams charged 91 defendants in eight cities for their alleged participation in a Medicare fraud scheme involving more than $290 million in false billings.
- From September 28 through September 30, DOJ hosted a three day health care fraud training conference for approximately 175 federal prosecutors, FBI agents, HHS/OIG agents, and others.
- Continued a series of regional fraud prevention summits around the country to improve the exchange of information with partners in the public and private sector and educate beneficiaries, providers, and the public to better identify and prevent health care fraud. Summits were held in Brooklyn (November 2010), Boston (December 2010), Detroit (March 2011), and Philadelphia (June 2011).

In addition to the activities of HEAT, CMS and law enforcement agency representatives, such as members of the Civil and Criminal Divisions, the USAOs and Executive Office for United States Attorneys (EOUSA), the FBI, and HHS/OIG, have met on a periodic basis through numerous local or regional health care fraud working groups and task forces.

EOUSA and CMS also sponsor a monthly national conference call during which Assistant United States Attorneys (AUSAs) from all districts have the opportunity to interact directly with CMS representatives, receive timely reports on CMS operations, and obtain answers to questions related to specific issues regarding current investigations. The Departments also convene interagency staff-level working groups as needed to develop mutual proposals for improving our health care fraud fighting capabilities.

In addition, attorneys from HHS/OIG have been detailed to the Fraud Section of the Criminal Division as Special Trial Attorneys and to USAOs as Special Assistant U.S. Attorneys to provide USAOs with additional prosecutorial resources.

During FY 2011, the many significant HCFAC Program accomplishments included the following:

Medicare Fraud Strike Force

The first Medicare Fraud Strike Force (Strike Force) was launched in March 2007 as part of the South Florida Initiative, a joint investigative and prosecutorial effort against Medicare fraud and abuse among Durable Medical Equipment (DME) suppliers and Human Immunodeficiency Virus (HIV) infusion therapy providers in South Florida. The Strike Force teams use advanced data analysis techniques to identify high-billing levels in health care fraud hot spots so that interagency teams can target emerging or migrating schemes along with chronic fraud by criminals masquerading as health care providers or suppliers. Based on the success of these efforts and increased appropriated funding for the HCFAC program from Congress and the Administration, DOJ and HHS expanded the Strike Force to include teams of investigators and prosecutors in a total of nine cities – Miami, FL; Los Angeles, CA; Detroit, MI; Houston, TX; Brooklyn, NY; Baton Rouge, LA; Tampa, FL; Chicago, IL; and Dallas, TX. The Departments plan to expand the Strike Force teams where Medicare claims data reveal aberrant billing patterns and where intelligence data analysis suggests that fraud may be occurring, contingent on available resources.

Each Medicare Fraud Strike Force team combines the data analysis and administrative action capabilities of CMS, the investigative resources of the FBI and HHS/OIG, and the prosecutorial resources of the Criminal Division's Fraud Section and the USAOs. Strike Force accomplishments from cases prosecuted in all nine cities during FY 2011 include[11]:

- 132 indictments, informations and complaints involving charges filed against 323 defendants who allegedly collectively billed the Medicare program more than $1 billion;
- 172 guilty pleas negotiated and 17 jury trials litigated, winning guilty verdicts against 26 defendants; and
- Imprisonment for 175 defendants sentenced during the fiscal year, averaging more than 47 months of incarceration.

In the four and a half years since its inception, Strike Force prosecutors filed more than 600 cases charging more than 1,150 defendants who collectively billed the Medicare program more than $2.9 billion; 663 defendants pleaded guilty and 74 others were convicted in jury trials; and 543 defendants were sentenced to imprisonment for an average term of nearly 42 months.[12]

Examples of successful cases initiated or concluded in districts where Strike Force prosecution teams were operational during FY 2011, as well as other successful cases, organized by provider or fraud type follow.

Phase 1: Miami (Southern District of Florida)

- In September 2011, the U.S. District Court in Miami sentenced the owner of a mental health care company (American Therapeutic Corporation, or ATC) to 50 years in prison for orchestrating a $205 million Medicare fraud scheme involving fictitious mental health services. The court also sentenced a co-owner to 35 years in prison and a third codefendant to 91 months in prison following guilty pleas to their roles in the scheme. The defendants paid kickbacks to assisted living facilities and halfway houses in exchange for patients being brought to ATC facilities so they could bill Medicare for intensive mental health treatments that were medically unnecessary or never provided. ATC pleaded guilty to the charges in April and May of this year.
- In June 2011, the U.S. District Court in Miami sentenced a physician to 235 months in prison for his role in a $23 million injection and HIV infusion scheme. The physician, who was convicted on multiple charges following a three-week trial, diagnosed almost all patients with the same rare blood disorders, which the patients did not have, and prescribed expensive medications to the patients for the sole purpose of receiving Medicare reimbursements. The court also found that the physician obstructed justice by testifying falsely at his trial, and that he caused a risk of serious bodily injury to his patients. The court sentenced the clinic's owner/operator to 82 months in prison. The two medical assistants, who falsified patient files to indicate that injection and infusion treatments were medically necessary, received 70 and 57 months in prison, respectively. The physician assistant, who instructed the clinic owner/operator as to which medications and in what amounts to bill Medicare to ensure that the clinic received the maximum reimbursement, was sentenced to 54 months in prison.
- In August 2011, the court sentenced a registered nurse employed by a Miami-Dade based home health care agency to 120 months in prison following a jury conviction in May for his role in the submission of

$230,000 in false claims to Medicare for services that were not medically necessary or actually provided to Medicare beneficiaries. Between 2007 and 2009, the nurse completed hundreds of documents in which he claimed that he had injected Medicare beneficiaries with insulin two times a day, seven days per week. Trial evidence, however, showed that some beneficiaries were neither in need of insulin nor homebound.

- In November 2010, the court sentenced an owner/operator of an HIV infusion clinic to 120 months in prison for her role in a $23 million HIV infusion Medicare scheme. The defendant hired a physician and caused the physician to order unnecessary tests, sign false medical analyses and diagnosis forms, and authorize treatments to make it appear that medical services were being provided to patients who were Medicare beneficiaries. The services included medically unnecessary injection and HIV infusion therapies. The defendant paid Medicare beneficiaries kickbacks to induce them to claim that they had received legitimate services at the clinic when in fact the HIV infusion services were either not provided or were not medically necessary. The defendant laundered the proceeds of the fraudulent Medicare claims by transferring thousands of dollars in proceeds to two shell corporations that the defendant owned and controlled.
- In December 2010, the owner and operator of a medical clinic in Miami was sentenced to 60 months in prison for his role in a $16.6 million Medicare fraud scheme. Another owner and operator was sentenced to 60 months in prison. The clinic allegedly provided unnecessary prescriptions, plans of care and medical certifications to Miami-area home health agencies in return for kickbacks and bribes, and falsified patient files to make it appear as if Medicare beneficiaries qualified for daily skilled nursing visits.

Phase 2: Los Angeles (Central District of California)

- In August 2011, a jury in Los Angeles convicted three defendants, a DME owner, his wife, and an employee, for their roles in billing Medicare $14.2 million in fraudulent DME claims after a two-week trial. According to trial evidence, the owner and his wife were pastors of a Los Angeles area church where they also operated a DME supply company. The defendants purchased fraudulent prescriptions and documents, including Medicare numbers and identities of beneficiaries, including dead beneficiaries, from illicit sources to bill

Medicare for expensive, high-end power wheelchairs and orthotics that were medically unnecessary or never provided. When it appeared that the owner would have to close the DME company due to an audit by Medicare, the owner persuaded his sister and a member of the church to allow him to use their names and identities to open two new fraudulent DME companies. After closing the first DME company, the defendants and their co-conspirators continued to operate the fraud scheme from the two new fraudulent DME companies. Two co-defendants pleaded guilty previously and three defendants were convicted at trial in August 2011. All five defendants await sentencing in 2012.

- In July 2011, a jury in Los Angeles convicted the co-owner of a DME company and a purported home health agency for his role in causing approximately $11.9 million in fraudulent DME billings and $8 million in fraudulent home health billings to Medicare. The DME co-owner and a second co-owner conspired with others to defraud Medicare by paying marketers for access to Medicare beneficiary information and fraudulent documents in order to submit and cause the submission of false claims to Medicare for DME and home health services that were not medically necessary, and that often were not provided at all. The second co-owner pleaded guilty prior to the trial to multiple health care fraud charges in connection with his participation in the scheme.
- In April 2011, the U.S. District Court in Los Angeles sentenced a patient recruiter to 57 months in prison for her role in a scheme to submit more than $1.2 million in false claims to Medicare. Trial evidence established that the patient recruiter worked the streets of low-income and senior living communities in Oakland to recruit Medicare beneficiaries for the purpose of filing false claims to Medicare for expensive power wheelchairs that the beneficiaries did not want, need, or use. Beneficiaries testified at trial that the defendant approached them on the street, at stores, or in the lobbies of their apartment buildings and offered to get them power wheelchairs from Medicare for free. The defendant photocopied the Medicare card and other identity information for each Medicare beneficiary. The defendant sold the beneficiaries' Medicare information to a co-conspirator for between $400 and $500 each. Over a four-year period, she recruited and sold the Medicare information of approximately 200 different beneficiaries. The court sentenced the co-conspirator in this

case, who sold the Medicare beneficiary information to Los Angeles area DME companies, to 46 months in prison.

Phase 3: Detroit (Eastern District of Michigan)

- In March 2011, the U.S. District Court in Detroit sentenced the owner/operator of a Detroit-area HIV infusion and injection therapy clinic to 120 months in prison, and his wife, a physician, to 97 months in prison, for their roles in a $2.3 million Medicare scheme. The owner/operator and his co-conspirators imported the concept of infusion fraud to Detroit from South Florida after increased law enforcement scrutiny in Miami by creating an outpatient clinic in Detroit for the sole purpose of defrauding Medicare, recruiting beneficiaries with kickbacks, and money laundering. According to evidence presented at trial, the physician recorded fictitious symptoms in the patient charts maintained by the clinic in order to justify expensive and exotic medications that the clinic billed to Medicare. Patients were prescribed medications at the clinic based not on medical need, but rather on what medications were likely to generate the highest Medicare reimbursement. Evidence at trial also showed that Medicare beneficiaries were not referred to the clinic by their primary care physicians, or for any legitimate medical purpose, but rather were recruited to come to the clinic through the payment of cash kickbacks and prescriptions for narcotic drugs. Three co-conspirators were sentenced to prison terms of 63 months, 37 months, and 10 months, respectively; and three other coconspirators were sentenced to serve probation or time served in pre-trial detention plus supervised release.
- In December 2010, the owner and vice president of a clinic that purported to specialize in physical and occupational therapy were sentenced to prison terms of 151 months and 108 months, respectively, for their roles in a $23 million Medicare fraud scheme. The owner instructed her staff to create false documents and to add those documents to medical files to make it appear that the clinic's therapists had performed physical and occupational therapy services when she knew they had not. When Congress enacted a cap on physical and occupational therapy services to control costs in January 2006, the defendants devised a scheme to avoid the cap by billing for psychotherapy services. The defendants launched a lobbying effort to repeal the cap, which included the clinic staff drafting letters and

petitions to Congress purportedly on behalf of Medicare patients. They then instructed the clinic's staff to bill Medicare for their lobbying efforts as psychotherapy evaluations and visits. Three other co-defendants pleaded guilty and were sentenced to probation.

- In October 2010, the court sentenced a patient recruiter and operator of a Detroit-area home health agency to 63 months in prison for his role in submitting fraudulent claims for home health care and physical and occupational therapy services they purported to provide to homebound Medicare beneficiaries. The defendant admitted that he became the exclusive beneficiary recruiter at the home health care agency and that he recruited hundreds of patients, who were neither homebound nor in need of physical therapy services, through the payment of cash kickbacks in exchange for their Medicare information and signature on medical documents. The defendant also admitted that he knew that the beneficiaries' Medicare information was used to bill Medicare for physical therapy that was medically unnecessary and/or never preformed. The court also sentenced a co-defendant who was an unlicensed medical assistant to 46 months in prison for his role the conspiracy. Ten co-defendants await trial and nine other co-defendants have pleaded guilty and await sentencing.
- In June 2011, an employee of an HIV infusion clinic was sentenced to 77 months incarceration for his role in a health care fraud and money laundering scheme. The individual recruited and paid Medicare beneficiaries to act as patients, and the patients, in return, signed medical documentation and reimbursement forms that the clinic could use to bill Medicare for services never rendered. Additionally, the individual owned a company which he used to launder over $400,000 in Medicare payments. He fled the United States to avoid being apprehended, but was arrested in the Dominican Republic on November 29, 2010, and transferred into custody of U.S. officials.
- In June 2011, the co-owner of two Michigan nerve conduction clinics was sentenced to 15 months incarceration for her role in a Medicare fraud scheme. Between September 2007 and June 2008, the individual and co-conspirators used the clinics to bill Medicare for unnecessary tests and services, including nerve conduction studies. Patient recruiters were paid $100 to $150 for every patient that was brought into the clinic, and the patients received $50 to $75 in exchange for subjecting themselves to the medically unnecessary tests.

Phase 4: Houston (Southern District of Texas)

- In May 2011, the U.S. District Court in Houston sentenced the owner of a Houston-area DME company to 84 months in connection with a $2 million Medicare fraud scheme. A DME company co-conspirator was sentenced to 70 months in prison. The DME owner admitted that she paid kickbacks, sometimes $1,000 per patient, to recruiters who brought patients to her DME company. The owner then billed Medicare for medical equipment that the patients either did not need or never received, including power wheelchairs and orthotic devices. A physician co-conspirator was sentenced to 41 months in prison. Two patient recruiters were sentenced to 46 months in prison.
- In February 2011, the court sentenced a DME owner/manager to 57 months in prison in connection with a $2.8 million conspiracy to commit health care fraud. The defendant billed Medicare for arthritis kits for more than 683 beneficiaries, some of whom were deceased. None of the beneficiaries interviewed knew of the defendant, the co-defendant, or the DME provider. The sentencing of a physician co-conspirator, who signed purported prescriptions ordering DME that served as the basis for the owner's fraudulent claims to Medicare, remains pending. A third co-conspirator who was charged in a separate case pleaded guilty in August and is awaiting sentencing.
- In November 2010, the court sentenced a manager of a Houston-area DME company to 120 months in prison for his role in a $1.1 million Medicare fraud scheme. The defendant submitted false claims to Medicare for power wheelchairs and accessories as catastrophe-related in connection with Hurricanes Katrina, Rita, Ike, and Gustav. Many of the Medicare beneficiaries, including some who testified at trial, had never owned a power wheelchair during these catastrophes or had owned one that was damaged during these catastrophes. According to trial evidence, the defendant was previously convicted of fraud, and he failed to admit that previous conviction on documents he submitted to Medicare. A co-defendant who was a DME delivery driver was sentenced to 41 months in prison for delivering medically unnecessary DME, including power wheelchairs, to Medicare beneficiaries whom he knew did not need, and in some cases did not even want, the DME.
- In January 2011, a physician and five other individuals in Texas were sentenced to 41 months, 21 months, 26 months, 46 months, 70 months, and 41 months of incarceration, respectively, for their roles in

a multi-million dollar DME fraud scheme. Two others were sentenced to 10 months of community and home confinement and 3 years of probation, respectively. Evidence presented at trial showed that from 2003 to 2009, these individuals billed Medicare for fraudulent DME, including power wheelchairs and orthotic devices. The physician ratified prescriptions for medically unnecessary DME, while others created fraudulent patient files, paid kickbacks to recruiters, and delivered DME, such as power wheelchairs and orthotics, to beneficiaries who had no medical need for the equipment. The owner of the DME supplier and the other remaining defendants have pleaded guilty for their participation in various parts of the fraud scheme. Judicial proceedings continue for those individuals. This Medicare Fraud Strike Force investigation was a joint investigation with the Texas Medicaid Fraud Control Unit (MFCU).

Phase 5: Brooklyn (Eastern District of New York)

- In July 2011, a neurologist who owned and operated a Brooklyn medical clinic pleaded guilty for his role in a health care fraud scheme. The neurologist admitted that from January 2006 to December 2009, he caused false and fraudulent claims to be submitted to Medicare, the U.S. Department of Labor Office of Workers' Compensation Programs, New York State Workers' Compensation Board and Insurance Fund, and others. The defendant submitted claims for services that were not provided, misrepresented the services he provided by billing for a level of service higher than that which he performed, double billed different health care benefit programs for the same service provided to the same beneficiary, and billed for services purportedly performed when he was out of the country.
- In July 2011, a jury convicted two Brooklyn-area doctors of podiatric medicine on multiple health care fraud charges. Between January 2005 and March 2009, the defendants solicited Medicare and Medicaid beneficiaries and provided them with a variety of podiatric services. In many cases, beneficiaries came to the defendants' offices to have their feet cleaned and moisturized, and their toenails cut and cleaned with alcohol. The defendants then submitted, or caused to be submitted to Medicare and Medicaid, claims falsely billing for chemical cauterizations, a surgical procedure that involves

the burning of living tissue by a caustic chemical substance, when in fact those procedures were not necessary and had not been provided to beneficiaries.

- In May 2011, a Brooklyn physical therapist pleaded guilty for his role in a $11.9 million Medicare fraud scheme. Between January 2005 and July 2010, the physical therapist caused the submission of false and fraudulent claims to Medicare for physical therapy services that were not performed and were not medically necessary. In addition, the defendant hired individuals who were not certified as physical therapy assistants to purportedly provide physical therapy to Medicare beneficiaries.
- In February 2011, Strike Force prosecutors filed charges in the Eastern District of New York against seven defendants, including a physician, several medical clinic owners, and several ambulance drivers, for their roles in billing Medicare for $56.9 million in fraudulent claims. According to the indictment, the seven defendants allegedly paid kickbacks for Medicare beneficiaries to be transported by two ambulance services before billing Medicare for physical therapy and diagnostic tests that were medically unnecessary or not provided.

Phase 6: Baton Rouge (Middle District of Louisiana)

- In August 2011, following a two-week trial, a jury in Baton Rouge found guilty all four defendants in a $4.7 million Medicare fraud. Trial evidence established that between 2003 and 2009, the owner/operator of a Baton Rouge area DME company paid two patient recruiters to locate and solicit Medicare beneficiaries to attend "health fairs" hosted at churches and other locations. At the health fairs, doctors prescribed the beneficiaries power wheelchairs that were medically unnecessary. The DME owner then used the prescriptions to submit false and fraudulent claims to Medicare. The patient recruiters paid the doctors illegal kickbacks based on the number of power wheelchair prescriptions generated at the health fairs. The DME owner also paid kickbacks to the recruiters on a per prescription basis when beneficiaries received prescriptions for medically unnecessary power wheelchairs for which the owner's company fraudulently billed Medicare.
- In June 2011, the U.S. District Court in Baton Rouge sentenced an owner of a Baton Rouge DME company to 60 months in prison for his

role in a $5.4 million health care fraud scheme. The DME owner and three co-conspirators admitted to their roles in a multi-year scheme to defraud Medicare by routinely submitting claims to Medicare seeking reimbursement for a set of expensive braces (including a back brace, knee braces, and other items) when they knew that the braces were not medically necessary and had not been prescribed for the beneficiaries by their physicians. The court sentenced one coconspirator to 48 months in prison, a second to 30 months in prison, and another to 24 months probation.

- In January 2011, the court sentenced a DME owner/operator to serve 48 months in prison for his role in a $775,000 DME fraud scheme. The court sentenced the co-defendant, a physician, to 30 months in prison. The physician wrote prescriptions for medically unnecessary DME, such as power wheelchairs, wheelchair accessories, and feeding nutrients. The majority of the DME company's fraudulent claims were based on prescriptions for medically unnecessary DME that were written and provided by the physician.

Phase 7: Tampa (Middle District of Florida)

- In October 2010, the U.S. District Court in Tampa sentenced a physician and physician assistant to serve 108 months and 120 months in prison, respectively, for conspiring to defraud Medicare and for illegally prescribing controlled substances, primarily Oxycodone, Morphine, Hydrocodone, and Alprazolam. The court also ordered the forfeiture of the physician's Drug Enforcement Administration (DEA) Registrations and Florida Medical License, and forfeiture of the physician assistant's Florida Physician Assistant License. According to court documents, the physician allowed the prescribing of controlled substances to patients by unauthorized employees, including the physician assistant, without his presence, participation, and adequate supervision. The defendants used blank prescription forms signed by the physician. Many of these prescriptions were issued for controlled substances to patients without conducting adequate physical exams, making proper diagnosis, or considering alternative treatment options, and often with the knowledge that the patients receiving the controlled substances were misusing or abusing them, asking for drugs to support their own addictions, or sharing or giving the controlled substances away to others. Undercover detectives visited the clinic on six occasions, posing as patients and often asking for particular types of drugs; they were given prescriptions for those drugs with no medical basis and even after making clear that they had shared or intended to share the drugs with others. The physician assistant previously pleaded guilty in a separate, but related, case as an organizer and leader of an Oxycodone trafficking conspiracy and was sentenced to 120 months in prison to be served concurrently with the sentence in this case. The court sentenced a third co-defendant, who was an employee in the lead defendant's clinic, to 24 months in prison.

- In June and July 2011, five defendants pled guilty to conspiracy and other charges for their roles in a $757,000 scheme to defraud Medicare and were sentenced to prison terms ranging from 6 months to 46 months. According to court documents, three Miami-area residents and two other co-conspirators purchased an existing physical therapy business from its previous owners, along with the medical records of its patients, and used the names of a physical therapist and Medicare beneficiaries in the files without their permission. The defendants transformed the clinic into a fraudulent enterprise, purporting to provide physical therapy services to Medicare beneficiaries, but in reality used the stolen identities of a physical therapist and scores of patients to bill Medicare for physical therapy services that were never provided. According to court documents, from fall 2009 to summer 2010, the co-conspirators submitted and caused the submission of more than $757,000 in fraudulent claims to the Medicare program. The owner and president of the clinic admitted that he and his co-conspirators submitted claims to Medicare for physical therapy services that were never provided. The defendants also controlled corporate bank accounts into which Medicare deposited reimbursements based on the fraudulent claims. The reimbursements are alleged to have been transferred to the defendants, their coconspirators, and family members.
- In January 2011, the court sentenced two licensed physical therapists from Lakeland, Florida, a married couple, to 46 months and 42 months in prison, respectively, for making false statements in connection with health care benefits and aggravated identity theft. One defendant owned and the other defendant operated two companies in Lakeland that purported to provide physical therapy, speech therapy, and occupational therapy services to Medicare and Medicaid beneficiaries and recipients. According to court documents,

the defendants defrauded Medicaid by submitting fraudulent claims for reimbursement for services that were not performed by qualified, enrolled Medicaid providers, and falsely represented that the services were performed by qualified, enrolled Medicaid providers. They also submitted inflated claims and billed Medicaid for more services than were performed. They submitted claims for reimbursement for work they falsely claimed was performed on days when patients were not even present at their clinic and did not receive any treatment at all, and also submitted fraudulently created treatment notes during the course of the investigation.

Phase 8: Dallas (Northern District of Texas)

- In February 2011, Strike Force prosecutors filed an indictment charging the owner/operator of a DME supplier and her husband with conspiracy to commit health care fraud and five counts of health care fraud in connection with a $1.8 million Medicare fraud scheme. The indictment alleges that from September 2008 through December 2010, the defendants and other co-conspirators caused claims to be submitted to Medicare for DME that was never actually provided or was more expensive than the DME that was actually provided to beneficiaries. The defendants and co-conspirators submitted claims to Medicare for DME when, in fact, their company did not provide the equipment for which Medicare was billed. This case is scheduled for trial in January 2012.
- In February 2011, Strike Force prosecutors filed an indictment charging a CEO and Administrator of a home health care service and four co-defendants with conspiracy and kickback charges. A patient recruiter was also charged with paying and receiving health care kickbacks in connection with a $1 million Medicare fraud scheme. The CEO and his wife, as well as another CEO and his wife, paid kickbacks to a patient recruiter for referring Medicare patients to the home health service. From November 2008 through November 2010, the home health service billed Medicare for home health care when such services were not medically necessary and were not provided. This case is scheduled for trial in December 2011.

Phase 9: Chicago (Northern District of Illinois)

- In June 2011, a pharmacist pleaded guilty to charges filed in February that he fraudulently caused more than $200,000 in prescription drug claims to be paid by Medicare, Blue Cross Blue Shield of Illinois, and other private insurers for medications that were never dispensed to plan beneficiaries. The defendant owned the pharmacy through which he caused fraudulent claims for prescription medication to be submitted to health care benefit programs and pharmacy benefit management companies, when he knew that the pharmacy had not dispensed the prescription medications to the Medicare beneficiaries and private health plan subscribers.

- In June 2011, prosecutors filed an indictment charging a Chicago man who operated two home health care businesses, one of which was among the state's largest recipients of Medicare payments, on federal fraud charges for allegedly swindling Medicare of at least $20 million between 2006 and 2011. The defendant, who had no formal medical training, medical degrees, or licenses to practice as a health care professional, allegedly schemed with others to submit millions of dollars in false claims for reimbursement of home health care services purportedly provided to Medicare beneficiaries, which allegedly were never provided, were not medically necessary, or were inflated in price so that he and others could profit from the fraudulently-obtained funds. The defendant and his co-conspirators allegedly used the proceeds for various purposes, such as: using more than $5.5 million in cash to maintain lavish lifestyles, including gambling at casinos in the Chicago area and Las Vegas; buying automobiles, jewelry, and real estate in the United States and the Philippines; perpetuating the businesses by paying his employees and providing them with gifts; and bribing physicians and paying kickbacks to others in exchange for patient referrals.

Fraud by Pharmaceutical and Device Manufacturers and Related Individuals

- In October 2010, GlaxoSmithKline LLC (GSK) paid $600 million to resolve FCA allegations and related state claims in connection with its manufacturing and distribution of certain adulterated drugs made at GSK's now-closed Cidra, Puerto Rico, facility. In addition, SB Pharmco Puerto Rico Inc., a GSK subsidiary, pled guilty to a criminal felony for releasing into interstate commerce adulterated Kytril, Bactroban, Paxil CR, and Avandamet, in violation of the Food, Drug, and Cosmetic Act (FDCA) and paid a criminal fine of $150 million.

A criminal information charged that SB Pharmco's manufacturing operations failed to ensure that Kytril and Bactroban finished products were free of contamination from microorganisms. The criminal information further charged that SB Pharmco's manufacturing process caused Paxil CR two-layer tablets to split, which led the company to distribute tablets that did not have any therapeutic effect and tablets that did not contain any controlled release mechanism.

- In December 2010, Abbott Laboratories Inc., B. Braun Medical Inc., Roxane Laboratories, Inc., n/k/a Boehringer Ingelheim Roxane, Inc. and Dey, Inc., Dey Pharma, L.P., and Dey L.P., Inc., and affiliated entities paid $701 million to settle FCA allegations that they engaged in a scheme to report false and inflated prices for numerous pharmaceutical products knowing that federal health care programs relied on those reported prices to set payment rates. The actual sales prices for the products were far less than what defendants reported. By inflating the prices they reported to the drug pricing publications used by Medicare and Medicaid to set reimbursement rates, these manufacturers caused the government to set payment rates far above the actual prices paid to them by their customers, such as retail pharmacies. The manufacturers would then "market the spread" between the actual prices they charged their customers and the amount the government would later reimburse the customers in order to induce higher sales.
- In August 2011, Par Pharmaceutical, Inc. paid $90.9 million to resolve allegations that Par knowingly reported inflated drug prices and thereby caused the submission of false claims to the Medicaid program.
- In February 2011, the Irish pharmaceutical manufacturer Elan Corporation, PLC paid $60 million to resolve FCA allegations arising from its off-label marketing of the epilepsy drug Zonegran for a variety of uses other than those approved by the Food and Drug Administration (FDA) as adjunctive therapy for the treatment of partial seizures in epilepsy for adults over the age of 16. The United States alleged that this conduct caused false claims to be submitted to federal health care programs for off-label uses of the drug between April 2000 and April 2004. A subsidiary, Elan Pharmaceuticals, Inc., pled guilty to a misdemeanor violation of the FDCA. It paid a

criminal fine of $97 million and forfeited $3.6 million in substituted assets.

- In December 2010, Kos Pharmaceuticals, a subsidiary of Abbott Laboratories, paid more than $41 million to resolve criminal and civil liabilities arising from conduct relating to its drugs Advicor and Niaspan. The civil settlement resolved allegations that Kos offered and paid doctors, other medical professionals, physician groups, and managed care organizations illegal kickbacks in the form of money, free travel, grants, honoraria, and other valuable goods and services in violation of the Anti-Kickback Statute (AKS) to get them to prescribe or recommend Niaspan and Advicor. In addition, the settlement resolved allegations that Kos promoted the sale and use of Advicor for use as first-line therapy for management of mixed dyslipidemias (a disruption of the lipids in the blood), a use not approved by the FDA. As part of the global resolution, Kos also entered into a DPA and agreed to the filing of a criminal information charging the company with one count of conspiracy to violate the AKS.
- In June 2011, UCB, Inc. paid $34.4 million to resolve criminal and civil FCA liability arising from the illegal marketing of the epilepsy drug, Keppra, for off-label uses that were not medically accepted indications and ineligible for coverage, including headache, migraine, pain, bipolar, mood disorders, and anxiety. Under the terms of a separate criminal agreement, UCB pled guilty to one count of misdemeanor misbranding under the FDCA and paid an $8.6 million criminal fine.
- In June 2011, Novo Nordisk paid $25 million to resolve allegations that it engaged in off-label promotion of NovoSeven, a recombinant biologic drug that is FDA approved to treat hemophilia. The United States alleged that Novo Nordisk paid military physicians remuneration for questionable research to support and promote the use of NovoSeven for use in trauma-related hemorrhage, even in the face of mounting evidence of harm. As part of the settlement, the defendant has agreed to enter into an expansive Corporate Integrity Agreement (CIA) with HHS/OIG.
- In October 2010, Synthes, Inc., a major international medical device manufacturer, pled guilty to a criminal violation of the FDCA by introducing into interstate commerce medical devices that were adulterated and misbranded. Its subsidiary, Norian Corp., pled guilty to 110 criminal FDCA counts for related conduct and also pled guilty

to one felony count of a multi-object conspiracy including to defraud the United States and its agencies by impeding, impairing, and defeating the lawful functions of the FDA to protect the health and safety of the public. The corporate defendants paid more than $23 million in criminal fines, forfeiture, and other penalties. From May 2002 until fall 2004, the defendants conducted unauthorized clinical trials of Synthes medical devices in surgeries to treat vertebral compression fractures of the spine (VCF), a painful condition commonly suffered by elderly individuals. These surgeries were performed despite a warning on the FDA cleared label for the device against this use, and in the face of serious medical concerns about the safety of the devices when used in the spine. Before the marketing program began, pilot studies showed the company that the bone cement reacted chemically with human blood in a test tube to cause blood clots. The research also showed, in animals, that such cement caused clots became lodged in the lungs. The company did not stop marketing the product until after a third patient had died on the operating table. After the death of the third patient in January 2004, Norian and Synthes did not recall the product from the market – which would have required them to disclose details of the three deaths to the FDA – but, instead, compounded their crimes by carrying out a cover-up in which they made false statements to the FDA during an official inspection in May and June 2004. The companies also agreed to a $138,000 civil settlement for submission of claims to various health care programs resulting from the use of the company's bone cement in VCFs when such use was neither reasonable nor necessary, and such unapproved use was explicitly warned against. On November 21 and December 13, 2011, four former executives with Synthes, Inc., were each sentenced to terms of imprisonment. Two were each sentenced to nine months in prison; one was sentenced to five months, and the fourth to eight months. All four previously pleaded guilty to one misdemeanor count of shipping adulterated and misbranded Norian XR in interstate commerce. Three of the sentences were above the guidelines range of 0-6 months, but the court found the conduct of the executives, which resulted in at least three patient deaths, so egregious as to warrant an upward variance. Each was also sentenced to pay a $100,000 fine.

- In September 2011, Guidant LLC, a wholly owned subsidiary of Boston Scientific Corp. of Natick, MA, paid the United States $9.3 million to resolve FCA allegations that the company inflated the cost of replacement pacemakers and defibrillators to federal health care programs by knowingly failing to grant warranty credits and rebates to hospitals for pacemakers and defibrillators that were explanted while covered under a product warranty or another credit program.

Hospital Fraud

- In December 2010, privately-owned Archbold Memorial Hospital, Inc. ("Archbold"), of Thomasville, GA, paid $13.8 million to resolve FCA liability related to allegations that from November 2002 through July 2008, it made false representations to the Georgia Department of Community Health, the agency that administers the Medicaid program in that state, that it was a public hospital in order to participate in the Medicaid Upper Payment Limit (UPL) program and to receive additional Disproportionate Share Hospital (DSH) program funds that are not available to private hospitals.
- In January 2011, seven hospitals paid $6.3 million to resolve FCA liability related to kyphoplasty claims. The settling facilities included: Lakeland Regional Medical Center, Lakeland, FL; The Health Care Authority of Morgan County – City of Decatur dba Decatur General Hospital, Decatur, AL; St. Dominic-Jackson Memorial Hospital, Jackson, MS; Seton Medical Center, Austin, TX; Greenville Memorial Hospital, Greenville, SC; Presbyterian Orthopaedic Hospital, Charlotte, NC; and The Health Care Authority of Lauderdale County and the City of Florence, AL, d/b/a the Coffee Health Group, f/k/a Eliza Coffee Memorial Hospital. The settlements resolved allegations that each hospital overcharged Medicare from 2001 to 2008 by performing kyphoplasty, a minimally-invasive procedure used to treat certain spinal fractures, on an inpatient basis. The procedure can be performed safely as an outpatient procedure, but the government alleged that the settling hospitals performed the procedure on an inpatient basis in order to increase their Medicare billings.
- In November 2010, Simi Valley Hospital in Simi Valley, CA paid $5.2 million to resolve FCA allegations related to billing outpatient detoxification services as inpatient psychiatric care. The United States

alleged that Simi Valley Hospital submitted false claims for inpatient psychiatric care to Medicare from 1996-2000.

- In September 2010, Santa Clara Valley Medical Center (SCVMC) agreed to pay $4.3 million to resolve its liability under the FCA in connection with improper billing for one-day hospital admissions that did not meet medical necessity criteria for inpatient services. SCVMC is an acute-care hospital owned and operated by the County of Santa Clara, CA. SCVMC disclosed through the OIG Self Disclosure Protocol that it had billed Medicare and Medi-Cal for one-day inpatient hospital stays which, instead, should have been billed as outpatient observation services.
- In April 2011, AHS Hillcrest Medical Center LLC; AHS Tulsa Regional Medical Center LLC, Ardent Health Services LLC; and Ardent Medical Services, Inc. (collectively the Ardent Entities) entered into a FCA settlement agreement and agreed to pay $3.9 million to resolve allegations that, between January 2003 and December 2009, the Ardent Entities caused false claims to be submitted to Oklahoma Medicaid. Specifically, the Children and Adolescent Behavioral Health Services Unit of the Tulsa Regional Medical Center (renamed Oklahoma State University Medical Center in 2006) allegedly failed to provide inpatient psychiatric services to patients under the age of 21 in the intervals of time required by state regulations. Instead, shorter therapy sessions were allegedly provided and documented as if they had been appropriately provided. In connection with this settlement, AHS Hillcrest Medical Center, which assumed ownership and operation of the Unit in 2009, entered into a five-year CIA. The CIA obligations include oversight by a board of directors and an Independent Review Organization's review of the Unit's claims and quality control systems.
- In April 2011, North Carolina-based Rex Healthcare paid $1.9 million in order to resolve FCA liability related to a variety of medically unnecessary inpatient admissions, including those related to kyphoplasty procedures. The settlement resolved allegations that the hospital overcharged Medicare from 2001 to 2008 for a variety of minimally-invasive procedures performed on an inpatient basis despite any medical need for more costly inpatient care. The government alleged that Rex Hospital performed the procedures on an inpatient basis in order to increase their Medicare billings.

- In September 2010, Christus Health and seven of its hospitals (collectively, Christus) agreed to pay $970,987 to resolve their civil liability for allegedly violating the FCA, the Civil Monetary Penalties Law (CMPL), and certain common law causes of action. Christus is a health system that operates hospitals throughout the southwestern United States. At the advice of a consulting firm, Healthcare Financial Advisers (HFA), Christus allegedly filed inflated cost reports. HFA allegedly prepared and Christus filed cost reports that sought reimbursement for various categories of items of unallowable costs, while simultaneously preparing a second set of cost reports, which more accurately represented the amount of reimbursement to which the hospitals were entitled. In addition to the settlement amount, Christus also refunded to Medicare a $649,210 overpayment which it received as a result of improperly seeking reimbursement for unallowable costs on past cost reports.
- In April 2011, Masonicare Health Center (Masonicare) agreed to pay $447,776 to resolve its liability for allegations under the FCA. The settlement agreement resolved allegations that Masonicare improperly overcharged the Medicare and Medicaid programs from January 1, 2001 through May 31, 2010 for Lupron injections, which are commonly used to treat prostate cancer in men and manage endometriosis in women. Using the health care procedure coding system (HCPCS), Masonicare allegedly billed Medicare and Medicaid for Lupron injections provided to its male patients under an HCPCS code designated for female beneficiaries, which is reimbursed at double the rate. HHS/OIG reserved its right to exclude the entity.
- In November 2010, St. John's Health System (St. John's) agreed to pay the United States $318,364 to resolve its liability under the FCA for submitting fraudulent claims to Medicare and Medicaid for psychotherapy services. The settlement resolves allegations that, from January 1, 2005 through December 31, 2008, St. John's billed for multiple units of psychotherapy services under the code for group medical psychotherapy. The Federal government contends that the services that were provided were not psychotherapy sessions, but group counseling meetings, including Alcoholics Anonymous meetings provided by unqualified professionals. The settlement also resolved allegations that St. John's billed for services provided by lower-level practitioners without using modifiers to indicate who

provided the services, resulting in a 25 percent higher payment under Medicare and Medicaid.

Fraud by Physicians

- In June 2011, a physician in Las Vegas, Nevada, paid the United States $5.7 million to settle allegations that he submitted false claims to Medicare, TRICARE, and the Federal Employees Health Benefits Plan (FEHBP). The United States alleged that the defendant upcoded various radiation oncology services, unbundled several procedures affiliated with radiation treatment plans, and billed for other medically unnecessary radiation oncology services.
- In February 2011, a Missouri physician pled guilty to health care fraud and conspiracy to distribute OxyContin and oxycodone. The defendant admitted that he participated in a conspiracy with others, who have also pled guilty to distributing OxyContin and oxycodone from July 2006 to January 2010 and are awaiting sentencing. The defendant began operating a mobile physician business to make house calls to hotels and businesses, but used the business to write prescriptions for Schedule II controlled substances for individuals without a medical examination or medical need. The defendant agreed to forfeit $1.2 million which represented the proceeds from a drug-trafficking conspiracy and health care fraud. He also agreed to relinquish his Missouri and Kansas medical licenses.
- In December 2010, a Grand Rapids dermatologist was sentenced to 120 months in prison following his jury conviction on 31 counts of health care fraud. The charges in the indictment involved the upcoding of a variety of dermatological procedures and the fraudulent billing of office services for skin diseases that did not exist. The evidence at sentencing included expert testimony that many patients had undergone unnecessary surgical procedures to have benign skin lesions removed in order to fuel the dermatologist's various fraud schemes. The investigation and prosecution also revealed that the dermatologist had reused sutures on multiple patients, resulting in the notification and testing of thousands of patients for HIV and Hepatitis C by the county health department.
- In May 2011, a Florida physician was convicted of 17 counts of health care fraud and 126 counts of unlawful dispensing of controlled substances. At trial, the government presented evidence that, while operating a medical business, the physician prescribed controlled

substances to patients without sufficient medical necessity, and did so in quantities and dosages that caused his patients to abuse, misuse, and become addicted to the drugs. Through the testimony of more than 76 witnesses, the government established that the defendant continued to prescribe controlled substances even after he learned that the patients were addicted to the drugs, had suffered overdoses from them, were doctor shopping to get more drugs, or were, in some cases, selling the drugs on the street. The jury's verdict included a finding that the defendant's dispensing of controlled substances resulted in the deaths of two patients. The defendant faces a maximum sentence of 10 years imprisonment for each of the health care fraud convictions, a sentence of up to 20 years imprisonment on each of the controlled substance dispensing counts, and a mandatory 20 years to life term of imprisonment on the one count of dispensing a controlled substance resulting in death.

- In November 2010, an Arkansas doctor, affiliated with d/b/a Arkansas Center for Women, was convicted of health care fraud and misbranding. The indictment charged the defendant with obtaining Mirena intrauterine devices ("IUDs"), which were not approved by the FDA, from outside the United States via Canadian pharmacy websites for approximately half the cost of the FDA-approved IUDs. The defendant provided the IUDs to patients and billed the Arkansas Medicaid Program, as well as private insurance companies and self-pay patients, as if patients were provided with the more expensive, FDA-approved version of Mirena.

Fraud by Other Practitioners

- In November 2010, a surgical monitoring company and its former President and CEO agreed to pay more than $2.7 million to resolve allegations that the company fraudulently billed Medicare for intra-operative monitoring services provided to hospital patients undergoing complex surgical procedures. Intra operative monitoring services are used to help reduce the risk of complications during surgery by identifying changes in the brain, spinal cord, and peripheral nerve function prior to irreversible damage. The government's investigation found that the physicians employed by the company were improperly billing for monitoring multiple surgeries at one time and were billing for more time than they had actually spent monitoring the surgeries. In addition to paying almost

$2.8 million to resolve this matter, the former President and CEO agreed to a three-year voluntary exclusion from all federal health care programs.

- In September 2010, a formerly licensed nurse in Puerto Rico was sentenced to 18 months of incarceration after pleading guilty to four counts of misbranding of a drug with the intent to defraud. Though not licensed as a physician, this individual presented himself as a physician specializing in wound care, treated several beneficiaries suffering from skin ulcers, and regularly provided patients with prescriptions for medications to treat such conditions. These pharmacy claims were paid by health care benefit programs, including Medicare Advantage (MA) plans. When writing the fraudulent prescriptions, the nurse used his expired U.S. Virgin Islands nursing license number, which matched that of a legitimate Puerto Rican physician with no knowledge or involvement in the scheme. This case involved HHS/OIG and FDA's Office of Criminal Investigations.

Fraud by Pharmacies

- In April 2011, CVS Pharmacy paid the United States and 10 states $17.5 million to resolve FCA allegations that CVS submitted inflated prescription claims to the government by billing the Medicaid programs in Alabama, California, Florida, Indiana, Massachusetts, Michigan, Minnesota, New Hampshire, Nevada, and Rhode Island for more than what CVS was owed for prescription drugs dispensed to Medicaid beneficiaries who were also eligible for benefits under a primary third party insurance plan (excluding Medicare as the primary payor). The United States alleged that rather than billing the government for what the insured would have been obligated to pay had the claims been submitted solely to the third party insurer (typically the co-pay), CVS billed and was paid a higher amount by Medicaid.
- In September 2010, Specialized Pharmacy Services, which provides services to residents of long term care facilities, agreed to pay $11.6 million, and entered into a settlement agreement with the state of Michigan to resolve allegations that from 2002 to 2009 it charged Medicaid a greater amount for prescription medications than it did private insurance companies. Under Michigan law, a pharmacy cannot bill Medicaid more than it customarily accepts from a private health

insurer for prescription medications. This case was jointly investigated with the Michigan MFCU.

- In December 2010, Woodhaven Pharmacy Services, Inc., d/b/a Remedi Seniorcare, a long term care pharmacy company located in Baltimore, Maryland, paid the United States $1.3 million to settle claims that it violated the FCA by failing to credit federal programs and Medicaid for medications that were dispensed to patients in long term care facilities and later returned and re-dispensed to other nursing home and assisted living patients.
- In January 2011, CVS Pharmacy, agreed to pay $969,230 to resolve liability under the FCA for billing federal health care programs for services provided by excluded individuals. From September 20, 2005 through July 31, 2009, three CVS Pharmacy stores in New York and New Jersey allegedly submitted or caused to be submitted to the TRICARE and Medicare programs claims for prescription drugs that were dispensed by an excluded pharmacist. The pharmacist was excluded in 2004 from participating in federal health care programs based on his conviction for attempted criminal sale of a controlled substance in New York.
- In April 2011, eTEL-Rx, Inc., (eTEL-Rx), a pharmacy that provides drugs to nursing home facilities throughout the state, entered into a settlement agreement which included restitution in the amount of $650,000 to resolve its alleged liability under the civil FCA. Between January 1999 and December 2007, eTEL-Rx allegedly billed Medicaid directly for medications and nutritional supplements of terminally ill patients that should have been billed to the appropriate hospice providers. In addition, eTEL-Rx accepted the return of unused drugs paid for by Medicaid without crediting Medicaid for the returns. They subsequently re-dispensed the returned drugs, resulting in Medicaid paying eTEL-Rx again for the drugs already reimbursed by Medicaid. As part of the settlement, eTEL-Rx entered into a CIA with OIG.

Fraud by Clinics

- In April 2011, Dartmouth Hitchcock Clinic, Mary Hitchcock Memorial Hospital, and related entities (collectively Dartmouth), agreed to pay $2.2 million to resolve its liability under the FCA for allegedly submitting improper claims to Medicare, Medicaid, TRICARE, and the Veteran's Administration. Between February 1,

2001 and September 30, 2007, Dartmouth's Anesthesiology Department (AD) allegedly submitted improper claims for services not supervised by attending physicians in the AD's Pain Clinic, submitted improper claims for services not supervised by attending physicians related to bedside procedures, and submitted improper claims for time based billings in the AD's Critical Care Unit. According to federal regulations and related guidelines, physicians are allowed to bill for certain services provided by residents, but only if those services are performed while a physician is present and the medical record documents physician presence.

- In August 2011, the United States entered into a settlement agreement for $1.4 million with Treehouse Pediatric Clinic of Texas and related entities, to resolve allegations that the clinic presented claims for payment with TRICARE for services provided to autistic children by non-certified, unlicensed behavioral therapists. As a condition for payment, TRICARE's rules and regulations specifically required that these services be provided by licensed behavioral therapists. In filing claims, the licensed provider represented that she alone provided one-on-one behavioral therapy, when, in fact, unlicensed and unsupervised persons provided the therapy to the children.

Fraud by Medical Equipment Suppliers

- In May 2011, the United States District Court for the Middle District of Tennessee entered a judgment of $82.6 million in favor of the United States in a FCA case alleging that Renal Care Group (RCG), Renal Care Group Supply Company (RCGSC) and Fresenius Medical Care Holdings, Inc. violated the FCA when they submitted claims from 1999 through 2005 to the Medicare program for home dialysis supplies provided to patients with end stage renal disease (ESRD) for reimbursement of the supplies and equipment. All of these claims, as well as related claims for support services rendered by RCG dialysis clinics were false because the defendants were prohibited from and not qualified to bill Medicare for these home dialysis patients. Under Federal law, the Medicare program pays companies that provide dialysis supplies to ESRD patients only if the companies that provide the supplies are truly independent from dialysis facilities and the ESRD patient chooses to receive supplies from the independent supply company. The government alleged that the defendants set up a sham billing company, RCGSC, which was not independent from

RCG. Further, RCG interfered with ESRD patients' choice of supply options, requiring patients to "move" to RCGSC. Even after RCG employees raised concerns and industry competitors closed their supply companies, RCG kept RCGSC open because of the illicit revenue it created.

- In September 2011, Hill-Rom Company, Inc (Hill-Rom), a national DME supplier, paid the United States $41.8 million to resolve allegations that Hill-Rom submitted false Medicare claims for bed support surfaces for patients who no longer needed or were no longer using this DME. Bed support surfaces are generally used to relieve pressure on bed-bound patients suffering wounds or other sores.
- In April 2011, a former officer of Rikco International paid $27 million to resolve FCA allegations that it sold shoe inserts for diabetic patients that did not conform to Medicare's requirements for those products. Also, as part of the global resolution of this matter, the defendant also agreed to plead guilty to a felony charge of mail fraud for this conduct. Despite being advised that the inserts did not conform to Medicare's requirements, the defendant continued to sell the non-compliant inserts in 2006.
- In May 2011, the owner and operator of a Florida pharmacy was sentenced to 52 months incarceration for health care fraud. Between August 2006 and April 2007, the individual used his pharmacy to submit false claims to Medicare, including claims for deceased beneficiaries. These claims sought reimbursement for the cost of DME prescription medications, and other items and services for Medicare beneficiaries in Florida that were not prescribed by doctors or provided as claimed.
- In May 2011, a Florida man was sentenced to 55 months incarceration for defrauding the Medicare program. Between July 2006 and January 2007, the individual, the owner of a DME supply company, caused the company to submit false and fraudulent Medicare claims for DME items such as pressure support ventilators, therapy pumps, and other DME that were not prescribed by physicians nor received by Medicare beneficiaries.
- In October 2010, a consent judgment was entered against a defendant for $657,708 for causing the submission of false claims by the defendant's former company Orthoscript, Inc. to Medicare, TRICARE, and FEHBP from 1999 through 2004. Orthoscript

improperly billed the programs under the wrong, higher paying codes for certain DME. The defendant was earlier tried and convicted for fraud in connection with the scheme.

Quality of Care

- In April 2011, Areté Sleep, LLC, Areté Sleep Therapy, LLC, and Areté Holdings LLC (collectively Areté), agreed to pay $650,000 in a settlement to resolve FCA allegations. Between November 2002 and December 2009, Areté allegedly made false claims to Medicare for diagnostic sleep tests performed by technicians in its Arizona and Texas facilities who lacked the licenses or certifications required by Medicare rules and regulations. The settlement also resolves allegations that Areté further submitted false claims for medical devices, such as continuous positive airway pressure devices, resulting from the uncertified technicians' tests.

Fraud by Nursing Homes

- In April 2011, Genesis Rehabilitation Services (GRS), an affiliate of Genesis HealthCare LLC, agreed to pay $1.5 million to resolve its liability under the FCA for allegedly submitting claims to Medicare and Medicaid for services provided by an unlicensed speech therapist. Between October 2006 and June 2010, GRS allegedly employed an unlicensed speech therapist who provided forged licenses and documentation to GRS in order to maintain her employment. GRS failed to verify the documentation. As a result, GRS routinely submitted claims to Medicare and Medicaid for services for licensed speech therapy services that were provided by an unlicensed therapist.
- In January 2011, Senior Care Group, Inc., of Tampa FL, agreed to pay the United States $953,375 to settle allegations that the nursing home company, which operated two skilled nursing facilities in the western mountains of North Carolina, defrauded the Medicare Part A program. Senior Care's rehabilitation contractor placed intense management pressure on employees to maximize billings, billed for services that were unnecessary and then forwarded the billings for those unnecessary services to Senior Care for submission to Medicare. As an example of the unnecessary services performed, occupational therapy to elderly Alzheimer's Syndrome patients who could never expect to return to the workforce was regularly provided. As a

condition of settlement, Senior Care was required to enter into a CIA with HHS/OIG under which the company will be monitored for a period of five years to ensure that the company does not commit fraud against government health care programs in the future.

Kickbacks and Self-Referrals

- In March 2011, Medline Industries, Inc. and The Medline Foundation paid the United States $85 million to resolve allegations that they improperly paid kickbacks to health care providers in violation of the FCA and the AKS. In particular, the settlement resolved allegations that Medline offered or paid unlawful remuneration to induce health care providers to purchase, lease, or order medical goods and supplies from Medline.
- In May 2011, Serono Laboratories, Inc., EMD Serono, Inc., Merck Serono S.A; and Ares Trading S.A. paid $44.3 million to resolve FCA allegations that, from January 2002 through December 2009, Serono paid health care providers kickbacks to induce them to promote or prescribe Rebif, a recombinant interferon injectable that is used to treat relapsing forms of multiple sclerosis. Serono is alleged to have made payments to providers for hundreds of speaker training meetings and programs, as well as payments for attending consultant, marketing, and advisory board meetings, all at upscale resorts and other locations.
- In December 2010, Detroit Medical Center, a non-profit company that owns and operates hospitals and outpatient facilities in Detroit, paid the United States $30 million after it reported to the government improper financial relationships with referring physicians. The physician self-referral law (Stark Law) and the AKS restrict the financial relationships that hospitals may have with doctors who refer patients to them. Most of the relationships at issue in this matter involved office lease agreements and independent contractor relationships that were either inconsistent with fair market value or not memorialized in writing.
- In November 2010, Ameritox Ltd. paid $16.3 million to resolve FCA allegations that the laboratory paid kickbacks to induce its physician clientele to refer drug testing services to the lab that were reimbursable by Medicare. In particular, the settlement resolves allegations that the Baltimore-based company made cash payments to physician clients to induce referrals from January 1, 2003 through

December 31, 2006, and that laboratory testing service offered collector personnel at no cost to the lab's physician clients in order to induce referrals from January 1, 2003 through June 30, 2010.

- In January 2011, St. Jude Medical Inc. of St. Paul, MN, paid the United States $16 million to resolve FCA allegations that the company used post-market studies and a registry to pay kickbacks to induce physicians to implant the company's pacemakers and defibrillators. Post-market studies are intended to assess the clinical performance of a medical device or drug after that device or drug has been approved by the FDA.
- Registries are collections of data maintained by a device manufacturer concerning its products that have been sold and implanted in patients. The United States contended that St. Jude used three post-market studies and a device registry as vehicles to pay participating physicians kickbacks to induce them to implant St. Jude pacemakers and defibrillators. Although St. Jude collected data and information from participating physicians, it is alleged that the company knowingly and intentionally used the studies and registry as a means of increasing its device sales by paying certain physicians to select St. Jude pacemakers and implantable cardioverter defibrillators for their patients. In each case, St. Jude paid each participating physician a fee that ranged up to $2,000 per patient. The United States alleged that St. Jude solicited physicians for the studies in order to retain their business and/or convert their business from a competitor's product.
- In April 2011, Cardinal Health, Inc. paid $8 million to settle FCA allegations that it paid two relators (a pharmacy owner and pharmacy consultant) substantial up-front payments to induce them to refer orders for prescription drugs to Cardinal Health in violation of the AKS and that the illegal inducement infected all claims submitted by the relators to Medicare, Medicaid, and other federal health care benefit programs and resulted in the submission of false claims to the United States.
- In October 2010, Wright Medical Technology, Inc. paid $7.9 million in a civil settlement agreement with the United States to resolve allegations that the company's fraudulent marketing practices caused false claims to be submitted to the Medicare program in violation of the FCA. The government alleged that Wright used consulting agreements with orthopedic surgeons as an inducement to use its artificial hip and knee reconstruction products. As part of the global

resolution, Wright entered into a 12 month Deferred Prosecution Agreement (DPA), consenting to institute and continue corporate compliance procedures and federal monitoring. The company has also entered into five-year CIA with HHS/OIG, which requires additional reforms and monitoring under HHS/OIG supervision.

- In September 2011, Ohio Valley Health Services and Education Corporation, a West Virginia company, paid the United States $3.8 million to settle claims that it engaged in improper financial relationships with referring physicians. The company operates hospitals in Wheeling, WV, and Martins Ferry, OH.
- In June 2011, Midtown Imaging, LLC and its former owners Midtown Imaging, P.A. and PBC Medical Imaging (collectively "Midtown Imaging") paid $3 million to resolve allegations that the radiology clinic violated the FCA and the Stark Law by submitting Medicare claims from 2000 through 2008 arising from certain leasing and professional services agreements with referring physicians and physician groups.
- In December 2010, Exactech, Inc. paid the United States $2.9 million to settle allegations that the company's fraudulent marketing practices caused false claims to be submitted to the Medicare program for its artificial hip and knee reconstruction products in violation of the civil FCA. As part of the global resolution, Exactech entered a 12-month DPA with the government, and the current Director of Sales for Exactech's Northeast Region pled guilty to conspiracy to violate the AKS.
- In November 2010, St. Elizabeth Medical Center (St. Elizabeth) agreed to pay $1.2 million to resolve its liability under the CMPL and the Stark Law. On January 23, 2009, St. Elizabeth disclosed through HHS/OIG's Self-Disclosure Protocol an improper billing arrangement for provider-based services involving a rural vascular outreach program that had occurred at one of the St. Luke Hospitals prior to its merger with St. Elizabeth. St. Elizabeth also disclosed several improper financial relationships between St. Luke and a referring physician involving the provision of free and below-fair-market-value space and support services without written agreements, which created potential liability under the Stark Law and the AKS.

Home Health Fraud

- In September 2011, Maxim Healthcare Services, Inc., one of the nation's leading providers of home health care services, executed a DPA, and agreed to pay more than $150 million, to resolve criminal and civil charges relating to a nationwide scheme to defraud Medicaid programs and the Veterans Affairs program. The settlement is the largest ever involving a home health care company. A related criminal complaint filed on September 12, 2011, alleges Maxim conspired to commit health care fraud in submitting more than $61 million in fraudulent billings to government health care programs for services not rendered or otherwise not reimbursable. The investigation revealed that the submission of false bills to government health care programs was a common practice at Maxim from 2003 through 2009. To date, nine individuals – eight former Maxim employees, including three senior managers, and the parent of a former Maxim patient – have pled guilty to felony charges arising out of the submission of fraudulent billings to government health care programs, the creation of fraudulent documentation associated with government program billings, or false statements to government health care program officials regarding Maxim's activities. During that time period, Maxim received more than $2 billion in reimbursements from government health care programs in 43 states. Provided Maxim meets all of the obligations set forth in the DPA, the agreement will expire in 24 months and the Complaint will be dismissed. The company has also entered into a five-year CIA with HHS/OIG, which requires additional reforms and monitoring under HHS/OIG supervision.
- In September 2011, LHC Group, Inc. paid the United States $65 million to resolve allegations that it violated the False Claims Act by submitting false home health care billings to Medicare, TRICARE, and the FEHBP. The company also agreed to be bound to the terms of a CIA with HHS/OIG. The settlement resolves claims that, between 2006 and 2008, LHC billed for home health services that were not medically necessary and for services rendered to patients who were not homebound.
- In November 2010, the two owners of a Mississippi home health agency were each sentenced to 120 months of incarceration for making false statements relating to a health care matter, theft of government funds, and conspiracy to commit money laundering.

Between 2001 and 2004, the agency submitted false claims for in-home physical therapy and physical medicine services to Medicare and Medicaid falsely purporting that the services had been rendered by a physician or a qualified employee under the physician's direct supervision when, in fact, they had not. The agency also inflated the time billed by claiming that beneficiaries received as many as 10 hours of therapy per session.

- In May 2011, Gentiva Health Services, Inc. (Gentiva) paid $12.5 million to settle allegations that it fraudulently billed Medicare for costs not covered by the program. Gentiva is a home health care service provider with over 200 agencies nationwide that provide skilled-nursing and home-health aide services to patients, many of whom are Medicare beneficiaries. Between 1998 and 2000, Gentiva allegedly improperly billed Medicare for salaries and other costs of employees performing sales designed to increase patient utilization of its services, which violates Medicare regulations.

Other Medicare/Medicaid Fraud

- In January 2011, CareSource, CareSource Management Group, Co., and CareSource USA Holding, Co., agreed to pay the United States and the state of Ohio $26 million to resolve allegations that, between January 2001 and December 2006, they caused Medicaid to make payments for health care services they failed to provide to children and adults with special health care needs and that they submitted false data to the state of Ohio so that it appeared they were providing these required services to improperly retain incentives received from Ohio Medicaid and to avoid penalties.
- In February 2011, BlueCross BlueShield of Illinois (BCBSIL), a division of Health Care Service Corporation, paid the United States and the state of Illinois $25 million to settle FCA and consumer fraud allegations. The settlement resolves claims by the United States that BCBSIL wrongly terminated insurance coverage for private duty skilled nursing care for medically fragile, technologically dependent children, in order to shift the costs of such care to the Medicaid program; Medicaid funds a special program designed to provide home care for children at risk of institutionalization. Children, whose specialized care should have been covered by BCBSIL under the terms of existing insurance policies, were shifted to the government-funded Home and Community Based Services Medicaid program. As

a result, Medicaid spent millions of dollars providing care that should have been paid for by private insurance.

- In November 2010, two defendants, and Medical Resources, LLC paid $22.6 million to resolve allegations that the defendants and MR caused America's Health Choice Medical Plans, Inc., a Medicare Advantage Organization (MAO), to falsely increase the severity of beneficiary diagnoses to obtain higher Medicare payments. Under MA, MAO's are paid more to provide services for members with serious and/or chronic medical conditions then they are for relatively healthy members.
- In February 2011, APS Healthcare agreed to pay $13 million to resolve FCA liability arising out of its Medicaid management contract with the state of Georgia. Under its Georgia Medicaid Management Program contract, APS Healthcare agreed to provide case and disease management services to Georgia Medicaid recipients and was paid a monthly fee for each member receiving such services. APS Healthcare resolved allegations that it submitted false claims to the Georgia Medicaid program because it did not provide those specialty services to Medicaid recipients.
- In June 2011, the City of Dallas agreed to pay $2.5 million and enter a three-year CIA to resolve its liability under the FCA related to allegations that it and ambulance billing company Southwest General Services of Dallas, LLC, improperly billed and obtained reimbursements from Medicare and Texas Medicaid for upcoded ambulance transports. The transports were provided by Dallas Emergency Medical Service between January 2006 and May 2010. HHS/OIG alleged that Dallas caused false claims to be submitted to federal programs that were improperly coded as Advanced Life Support, when, in fact, no such services were rendered and the patient did not require an Advanced Life Support transport.
- In September 2011, Universal American Corp., doing business in Wisconsin as Today's Health/ABRI, paid the United States $4.8 million to resolve allegations that, between January 1, 2007 and December 31, 2009, Universal American billed Medicare Part C for claims for beneficiaries in Wisconsin that resulted from violations of the Medicare Part C marketing regulations and the AKS. More specifically, the United States alleged that Universal American provided various forms of remuneration to physicians in exchange for referrals, made payments to beneficiaries in exchange for enrolling in

its Medicare Part C plan, provided misleading information to beneficiaries about the scope of coverage and benefits, and enrolled beneficiaries in its plan without their consent. As part of the settlement, the defendant agreed to enter into a CIA with HHS/OIG.

- In September 2011, Janzen, Johnston & Rockwell Emergency Medicine Management Services Inc. (JJ&R), a provider of billing services for physicians, hospitals, and other health care providers, paid the United States $4.6 million to settle allegations that it submitted false claims to Medicare and Louisiana's Medicaid program. In particular, the settlement resolves allegations that JJ&R inflated claims that it had coded on behalf of emergency room physicians in Louisiana and California.
- In April 2011, Dartmouth-Hitchcock Clinic and Mary Hitchcock Memorial Hospital in New Hampshire paid over $2 million to settle FCA claims that they knowingly submitted false claims to Medicare by billing the services of resident physicians, fellows, and others as if the services were provided by doctors, and by billing physician services as critical care services when in fact the services were not critical care services.
- In October 2010, Northwest Mobile Services, LLC, and Northwest Mobile Imaging (collectively, Northwest Mobile) agreed to pay $950,000 to settle allegations that they utilized unlicensed/unqualified x-ray technicians to provide x-ray services. Between January 2003 and July 2007, Northwest Mobile allegedly caused claims to be submitted to the Medicare program for services provided by x-ray technicians that did not meet formal education requirements for x-ray technicians.

Transportation Fraud

- In September 2011, American Medical Response, Inc. (AMR) agreed to pay $2.7 million plus interest and enter a five year CIA to resolve its liability under the FCA. This settlement resolves allegations that, between January 1, 2001, and December 31, 2005, AMR's three Brooklyn locations submitted upcoded claims for ambulance transportation services to federal health care programs. Upcoding occurs when a provider bills for a level of service higher than medically necessary. This was a joint investigation with the OIG for the Department of Veterans Affairs.

- In June 2011, two owners of a Texas ambulance transport business were sentenced to 108 months incarceration for submitting false claims to Medicare and Medicaid. Between January 2004 and November 2007, the owners submitted and instructed others to submit claims to Medicare and Medicaid to obtain reimbursements for transporting dialysis patients who did not meet the required criteria for ambulance transportation. This was a joint investigation with the Texas MFCU.
- In October 2010, the owner of two ambulance service suppliers in Texas was sentenced to 15 years of incarceration after being convicted of 12 counts of health care fraud, conspiracy to commit health care fraud, and money laundering. The ambulance service suppliers provided medically unnecessary transports of Medicare and Medicaid beneficiaries to and from dialysis treatments. This case was investigated jointly with the Internal Revenue Service (IRS), FBI, the Texas MFCU, and the Office of Personnel Management (OPM).

Other Fraud

- In September 2011, TriWest Healthcare Alliance Corp., a federal TRICARE program contractor that coordinates medical services for the military and their dependents, paid $10 million to resolve its potential liability under the FCA. The United States alleged that, between 2004 and 2010, TriWest frequently failed to give TRICARE, the benefit of discounts negotiated under "Letters of Agreement" (LOAs). TriWest entered into LOAs with medical providers to provide services at discounted rates to the government. Notwithstanding the LOAs, TriWest submitted claims to TRICARE at higher rates claimed by the providers, which TRICARE paid.

Department of Health and Human Services

Office of Inspector General

A certain portion of the funds appropriated under HIPAA are, by law, set aside for Medicare and Medicaid activities of HHS/OIG.[13] In FY 2011, the Secretary and the Attorney General jointly allotted $198 million to the HHS/OIG. Additionally, Congress appropriated $29.7 million in discretionary funding for HHS/OIG HCFAC activities.

HHS/OIG participated in investigations or other inquiries that resulted in 1,105 prosecutions or settlements in FY 2011, of which 995, or 90 percent, were health care cases. A number of these are highlighted in the Accomplishments section. In addition, during FY 2011, HHS/OIG excluded a total of 2,662 individuals and entities, the details of which are below.

Program Savings

Frequently, investigations, audits, and evaluations reveal vulnerabilities or incentives for questionable or fraudulent financial practices in agency programs or administrative processes. As required by the Inspector General Act, HHS/OIG makes recommendations to agency managers to address these vulnerabilities. In turn, agency managers recommend legislative proposals or other corrective actions that, when enacted or implemented, close loopholes and reduce improper payments or conduct. The savings from these joint efforts toward program improvements can be substantial. During FY 2011, HHS/OIG reported that legislative and administrative actions to make funds available for better use resulted in an estimated $19.8 billion in health care savings attributable to FY 2011 – $7.5 billion in Medicare savings and $12.3 billion in savings to the Federal share of Medicaid.

Additional information about savings achieved through such policy and procedural changes may be found in the HHS/OIG Semiannual Report, on-line at http://oig.hhs.gov.

Exclusions

One important mechanism for safeguarding the care provided to program beneficiaries is through exclusion of providers and suppliers who have engaged in the abuse or neglect of patients or fraud from participation in Medicare, Medicaid, and other federal health care programs. During FY 2011, HHS/OIG excluded a total of 2,662 individuals and entities. Among these were exclusions based on criminal convictions for crimes related to Medicare and Medicaid (1,015), or to other health care programs (233); for patient abuse or neglect (206); or as a result of licensure revocations (897). This list of conduct is not meant to be exhaustive, but identifies the most prevalent causes underlying HHS/OIG's exclusions of individuals or entities in FY 2011. Exclusion actions by HHS/OIG included:

- District of Columbia—The U.S. District Court for the District of Columbia affirmed HHS/OIG' s determination to exclude three former Purdue Frederick Co. executives: the former Chief Operating

Officer and Chief Executive Officer; the former Chief Scientific Officer; and the former General Counsel. The exclusions were based on the executives' convictions for their failure, as responsible corporate officers, to prevent or correct the fraudulent misbranding and distribution of OxyContin.

- Kentucky—An emergency medical technician was excluded for a minimum of 25 years based on her conviction for manslaughter. While under the influence of Methadone, the technician was driving an ambulance and swerved off the road striking a utility pole and chain link fence. The collision caused blunt force trauma to the patient that she was transporting, which caused the patient's death. The technician was sentenced to 10 years of incarceration. The Kentucky Board of Emergency Medical Services revoked her license to practice as an emergency medical technician.
- Pennsylvania—A physician was excluded for a minimum of 20 years based on his health care fraud conviction. Over a five year period, the physician submitted false and fraudulent claims to Medicare, TRICARE, FEHBP, and private insurers for treatment and services which were not rendered because he was not in the office or the patients were being treated by other physicians on the dates claimed. He was sentenced to one year and one day of incarceration and ordered to pay $1 million in restitution.
- Kansas—An osteopath and a licensed practical nurse were excluded for a minimum of 95 years each for their convictions related to conspiracy to commit health care fraud resulting in death, aiding and abetting the unlawful distribution of controlled substances resulting in serious bodily injury and death; unlawful distribution of controlled substances resulting in serious bodily injury; health care fraud resulting in death; health care fraud; and money laundering. The two, who are married, owned and operated a medical clinic which they used to distribute and dispense controlled substances illegally and defraud patients of money by operating it as, in essence, a prescription mill and a narcotics delivery system, commonly known as a "pill mill." The couple engaged in this scheme for a six-year period, during which numerous patients were hospitalized and numerous patients died due to overdoses of prescribed drugs. Additionally, they were previously ordered to pay restitution in the amount of $5 million and sentenced to 360 months and 396 months of incarceration, respectively.

- Oregon—A certified nurse assistant was excluded for a minimum of 35 years based on his convictions of sodomy, attempted rape, sexual abuse, and criminal mistreatment. The individual sexually abused two patients that were incapable of giving consent due to a mental disability. He was sentenced to 175 months of incarceration and his certificate to practice as a nurse assistant was revoked by the Oregon State Board of Nursing.
- Florida— On July 12, 2011, an HHS Departmental Appeals Board Administrative Law Judge (ALJ) upheld HHS/OIG's exclusion of the owner of a radiology company from participation in all federal health care programs under section 1128(b)(7) of the Social Security Act for eight years. The exclusion was based on the individual's submission of false claims to the Medicare and Medicaid programs for current procedural terminology code 36005, a procedural code that corresponds to injection for extremity venography. The procedure denoted by this code was never performed at the radiology company. Specifically, the ALJ found that the individual caused the submission of nearly 9,500 false claims to Medicare and Medicaid for reimbursement. DOJ previously entered into a civil FCA settlement with the individual and his radiology company.

Other Administrative Enforcement Actions – Civil Monetary Penalties

HHS/OIG has the authority to impose civil monetary penalties (CMPs) against providers and suppliers who knowingly submit false claims to the Federal government, who participate in unlawful patient referral or kickback schemes, who fail to appropriately treat or refer patients at hospital emergency rooms, or who engage in other activities prescribed in statute. HHS/OIG has continued to pursue its affirmative enforcement actions under these authorities. Examples include:

- North Carolina—Long Term Care, Inc. (LTC), a durable medical supplier, agreed to pay $170,000 to resolve its liability under the CMPL. LTC employed an excluded individual over a period of four years. LTC hired the excluded individual through a contract arrangement with a professional employment organization that provided human resources and staffing support to LTC.
- Florida—An orthopedic surgeon agreed to pay $101,000 to resolve his civil monetary penalty liability for allegedly soliciting kickbacks

from a medical device manufacturer. The government contends that the surgeon offered to leverage his product usage and ability to influence purchasing decisions through his position as Chief of Orthopedics at a hospital in exchange for a personal services contract worth a guaranteed $40,000.

- Alabama—Mobile Infirmary paid $45,000 to resolve allegations that it improperly refused to accept a patient transferred from another hospital. The patient came to the transferring hospital' s emergency room complaining of severe abdominal pain and required immediate specialized surgical intervention not available at the hospital. Mobile Infirmary allegedly refused to accept the transfer even though it had the capacity and specialized capabilities to treat the patient's condition. Ultimately, the patient was transferred to a hospital 60 miles away. The patient's condition deteriorated en route and he had to be transported by Life Flight helicopter to the receiving hospital, where he later died.
- Massachusetts— Beth Israel Deaconess Medical Center (Beth Israel) paid $233,932 to resolve its liability under the CMPL for allegedly submitting improper claims to Medicare for Lupron drug injections. Specifically, Beth Israel allegedly submitted claims for Lupron injections under a code that reimbursed at approximately double the rate as the code under which the claims should have been submitted.
- Florida— The owner of a medical supply company paid $124,141 to resolve his liability for allegations under the CMPL that he submitted false claims for diabetic shoe inserts through his DME company. The individual allegedly billed Medicare for custom molded diabetic shoe inserts but, in fact, provided prefabricated inserts to beneficiaries.

Audits and Evaluations

HHS/OIG conducts numerous audits and evaluations that disclose questionable or improper conduct in Medicare and Medicaid, and recommends corrective actions that, when implemented, correct program vulnerabilities and save program funds. Among these were:

Medicaid Rehabilitative Services Claims

HHS/OIG found that New York State improperly claimed an estimated $207.6 million in Federal Medicaid reimbursement for rehabilitation services submitted by community residence rehabilitation providers during calendar years (CY) 2004 through 2007. Of the 100 claims in the random sample, 31 complied with Federal and state requirements, but 69 did not. The deficient claims lacked one or more elements such as the required physicians' authorizations or reauthorizations for rehabilitation services, a service duration of at least 15 minutes, and/or a service plan reviewed and signed by a qualified mental health staff member. HHS/OIG recommended, among other things, that the state refund $207.6 million to the Federal government.

Medicaid Payment Error Rates

As a result of a review of the universe of claims submitted by four states to CMS for analysis under the Payment Error Rate Measurement (PERM), HHS/OIG found that CMS could not be assured that the PERM program produced a reasonable estimate of improper payments. For example, one state paid hospitals for inpatient or outpatient hospital services on a weekly basis, rather than a claim-by-claim basis. Therefore, CMS did not include these payments in its analysis of payment errors. For this, and other reasons, the states' Medicaid fee-for-service and managed care universes for the FY 2008 PERM program were or may have been incomplete or inaccurate. HHS/OIG recommended that CMS require the one state that was found not to be maintaining hospital payment information on a claim-by-claim basis to begin doing so for use in future PERM reviews and that CMS continue to work with all states, CMS Regional Offices, and statistical contractors on reconciling the PERM universes to state financial reports.

Prompt and Accurate Medicaid Payments

For FYs 2000 through 2008, HHS/OIG estimated that Indiana did not report Medicaid overpayments totaling $38.9 million (Federal share), as well as $39,000 (Federal share) in interest collected, in accordance with federal requirements. Federal law requires states to refund the Federal share of Medicaid overpayments. In addition, federal regulations require states to refund interest earned on overpayments before requesting additional federal funds. HHS/OIG recommended, among other things, that Indiana include unreported Medicaid overpayments of $61.6 million on the Form CMS-64, refund the $38.9 million Federal share, and develop and implement internal controls to correctly report and refund the Federal share of identified Medicaid overpayments and applicable interest.

HHS/OIG found that Illinois did not always comply with prompt-pay requirements for receiving the increased Federal Matching Assistance

Percentage (FMAP) under the American Reinvestment and Recovery Act. As a result, it improperly received approximately $2.6 million in increased FMAP from February 18, 2009, through September 30, 2009. The state agency's initial prompt-pay calculations included several inaccuracies related to the 30/90-day prompt-pay requirements and the inclusion or exclusion of certain claims in the daily prompt-pay compliance calculation. HHS/OIG recommended that the state refund $2.6 million to the Federal government for unallowable increased FMAP and ensure that calculations are performed in accordance with prompt-pay requirements.

Medicaid Family Planning Services

HHS/OIG conducted five separate audits of the claims by five states for Medicaid family planning services and found an aggregate overpayment of approximately $17.8 million (Federal share). The audits were of the family planning services provided during specified audit periods in Oregon, Kansas, Oklahoma, Colorado, and Washington state. The overpayments occurred because the claims for services did not meet state plan requirements, the services did not qualify for the enhanced 90 percent federal matching rate for family planning services, or the state submitted duplicate claims for the same service. HHS/OIG recommended, among other things, that the state return the identified overpayments to the Federal government.

Medicaid Personal Care Services

HHS/OIG issued several reports examining Medicaid payments for personal care services. Personal care services are services provided to the elderly, people with disabilities, and other individuals with chronic or temporary conditions and which permit them to remain in their homes. Such services typically assist with such activities as bathing, dressing, meal preparation, and grocery shopping, and are authorized under the Medicaid State plan or through a waiver approved by CMS.

HHS/OIG's 10-State review revealed that Medicaid paid about $724 million for personal care services claims that HHS/OIG determined were inappropriate because personal care attendants' qualifications were undocumented. These claims represented 18 percent of the total number of claims. The qualifications most often undocumented were background checks, age, and education. HHS/OIG estimated that Medicaid paid an additional two percent of claims inappropriately because the respondents had no record of providing services to the beneficiaries. Respondents were agencies or individuals that state Medicaid agency officials indicated

HHS/OIG should contact to request documentation to support attendants' qualifications. HHS/OIG reviewed claims paid from September 1, 2006 through August 31, 2007, and based upon that review recommended that CMS work with states to ensure that Medicaid claims for personal care services provided by attendants with undocumented qualifications are not paid and take action regarding the inappropriately paid claims identified in our review.

In six separate reports of personal care services (PCS) provided under the Medicaid programs in the States of North Carolina, New York, Nebraska, and Washington, and in the District of Columbia, HHS/OIG found that the states improperly claimed an aggregate $164 million (Federal share) in unallowable costs. HHS/OIG recommended, among other things, that the states refund the Federal share of the overpayments.

Medicaid Home and Community Based Services Waivers

HHS/OIG found that Pennsylvania improperly claimed a $2.1 million Federal share of Medicaid administrative costs for its Home and Community Based Services (HCBS) waiver for individuals aged 60 and over (Aging Waiver). Pennsylvania's Aging Waiver authorizes HCBS services for Medicaid beneficiaries aged 60 or older who are economically distressed and are clinically eligible for care in a skilled nursing facility. The $2.1 million was not allowable because the state did not identify the claimed costs in the Aging Waiver or its cost allocation plan. The state also could not support a $371,000 adjustment of a prior improper claim for training of skilled professional medical personnel. Finally, HHS/OIG set aside for further analysis and resolution $25.8 million Federal share of local agencies' administrative cost claims that were identified in the Aging Waiver, but not in the cost allocation plan and which may have included costs that did not benefit the Aging Waiver. HHS/OIG's recommendations included that Pennsylvania refund $2.1 million for administrative costs and $371,000 to correct the adjustment error. HHS/OIG also recommended that Pennsylvania work with CMS to resolve the $25.8 million in Federal share it claimed for local agencies' costs.

Medicaid School Based Services

HHS/OIG found that West Virginia was overpaid $22.8 million for the Federal share of school-based services because it included costs in the calculation of its rates that were not included in the reimbursement methodology described in the approved state plan. The errors occurred because the state did not provide adequate oversight of its consulting firm during the rate calculation process. HHS/OIG recommended that the state refund $22.8 million to the Federal government for FYs 2001 through 2003 and work with CMS to determine unallowable costs for FYs 2004 to the present, make the appropriate refund, develop more accurate school-based service rates, and make necessary revisions to the state plan.

Medicaid Services in an Adult Day Care Setting

HHS/OIG found that for the 12 State Medicaid programs that allow nursing- and therapy-focused adult day health services, approximately 43 percent of therapy services were provided by staff who lacked required supervision. Recommendations included directing states to enforce supervision requirements for staff who provide therapy services in Medicaid adult day health centers, specifying what services are required for Medicaid reimbursement of adult day health services, and taking appropriate action to address the service providers that did not respond to repeated data requests.

Medicaid Payments to State-Owned Hospitals

HHS/OIG found that Illinois improperly claimed an $82.9 million Federal share of payments it made to a State-owned psychiatric hospital that failed to demonstrate compliance with federal requirements. During the audit period, the hospital did not demonstrate compliance with special Medicare Conditions of Participation (CoP) because the state agency did not believe that doing so was necessary. HHS/OIG concluded, among other things, that Illinois should refund the $82.9 million.

Medicaid Hospital Outlier Payments

Eight state agencies reviewed by HHS/OIG did not calculate Medicaid inpatient hospital cost outlier payments in a way that would effectively limit the payments to extraordinarily high-cost cases. To protect hospitals against large financial losses from extraordinarily high-cost cases, state agencies may supplement base payments with an additional "outlier" payment. Medicaid outlier payments are calculated using formulas that vary by state. The states that were reviewed used outdated cost-to-charge ratios and did not reconcile Medicaid outlier payments upon settlement of cost reports. HHS/OIG recommended that CMS encourage all state agencies that make Medicaid outlier payments to use the most recent cost-to-charge ratios to calculate Medicaid outlier payments, reconcile Medicaid outlier payments upon cost report settlement or use an alternative method to ensure that outlier payments are more closely aligned with actual costs, and amend their state plans accordingly. The review is a follow-up to similar audits conducted in 2004.

Medicaid Drug Rebate Collections

For a covered outpatient drug to be eligible for Federal Medicaid funding under the program, the drug's manufacturer must enter into a rebate agreement with CMS and pay quarterly rebates to the states. HHS/OIG conducted several studies examining the collection of drug rebates. Among these were the following:

- In a nationwide follow-up to a 2005 review of Medicaid drug rebate programs, HHS/OIG found that many states still lack adequate assurance that all drug rebates due them are properly recorded and collected. HHS/OIG also examined the extent to which states had established controls over collecting rebates on single-source (brand name) physician-administered drugs, as required by the Deficit Reduction Act of 2005. HHS/OIG recommended continued emphasis on states submitting accurate and reliable information, placing priority on their billing and collecting of rebates, and collecting rebates for single-source physician-administered drugs.
- HHS/OIG estimated that California failed to invoice manufacturers for and collect $26.7 million ($13.6 million Federal share) in rebates for eligible compound drug ingredients for a 24-quarter period ending June 30, 2009. California's Rebate Accounting Information System was not designed to invoice rebates for compound drug ingredients, and its electronic claims for such expenditures did not comply with federal requirements related to invoicing manufacturers for rebates and reporting drug utilization data to CMS. HHS/OIG recommended, among other things, that California invoice manufacturers for the estimated $26.7 million in rebates and refund to CMS the Federal share of the rebates.
- HHS/OIG found that most of 49 responding states self-reported that they met or exceeded federal requirements to collect rebates for certain physician-administered drugs; however, 29 states reported difficulties with manufacturer nonpayment of rebates for the drugs. The states attributed the difficulty mainly to inaccuracies in the drug code information that providers entered on claims. Federal law requires that states collect rebates on all claims for certain physician-administered drugs for federal matching funds to be available.

HHS/OIG recommended five steps to ensure states' compliance with rebate-related requirements for physician-administered drugs, including working with states to develop guidance for implementing system edits that increase the efficiency of physician-administered drug claim reviews.

Medicare Program Investment Income

HHS/OIG found that the Medicare program loses potential savings associated with investment income that MA organizations earn between the time that they receive Medicare prepayments and the time that the MA organizations pay for medical services. HHS/OIG estimated that in CY 2007, MA organizations held Medicare funds for about 46 days before paying for medical services. The Medicare Part A and Part B Trust Funds (which finance the MA program) could have earned approximately $450 million of interest income in CY 2007 had prepayments to MA organizations been delayed until after the beginning of the beneficiary's coverage period by the same number of days that HHS/OIG estimated MA organizations held the Medicare funds. Alternatively, HHS/OIG estimated that Medicare could have saved about $376 million that 457 MA organizations earned in CY 2007 had federal requirements been established to require MA organizations to reduce their revenue requirements in bid proposals to account for anticipated investment income. HHS/OIG recommended that CMS evaluate the audit results and either pursue legislation to adjust the timing of Medicare's prepayments to MA organizations to account for the time that these organizations invest Medicare funds before paying providers for medical services, or develop and implement regulations that require MA organizations to reduce their revenue requirements in bid proposals to account for anticipated investment income.

Medicare Adverse Events

Of the nearly one million Medicare beneficiaries who were discharged from hospitals in October 2008, HHS/OIG found that an estimated one in seven (13.5 percent) experienced adverse events during their hospital stays. To establish an estimated adverse events incident rate, HHS/OIG included in our review: the National Quality Forum's Serious Reportable Events; Medicare hospital-acquired conditions (HAC); and events resulting in prolonged hospital stays, permanent harm, life-sustaining intervention, or death. The incidence rate projects to about 134,000 Medicare beneficiaries experiencing at least 1 adverse event in hospitals during a single month, with such events contributing to the deaths of a projected 15,000 beneficiaries. Physician reviewers determined that 44 percent of events were preventable, most commonly because of medical errors, substandard care, and inadequate patient monitoring and assessment. HHS/OIG recommended that the Agency for Healthcare Research and Quality and CMS broaden patient safety efforts to include all types of adverse events and enhance efforts to identify events. HHS/OIG also recommended that CMS provide more incentives for hospitals to reduce adverse events through its payment and oversight functions, including strengthening the Medicare HAC policy and holding hospitals accountable for adopting evidence-based practices.

Medicare Place-of-Service Coding for Physicians

In two separate reports, HHS/OIG found that two Medicare contractors overpaid physicians an estimated $28.8 million for incorrectly coded places of service during CYs 2008 and 2009. Physicians incorrectly used nonfacility place-of-service codes for services that were actually performed in facilities such as hospital outpatient departments or ambulatory surgical centers. To account for the increased overhead expense that physicians incur by performing certain services in nonfacility locations, Medicare reimburses physicians at a higher rate. However, when physicians perform these same services in facility settings, Medicare reimburses the overhead expenses to the facility, and the physician receives a lower reimbursement rate. Our recommendations included recovering the overpayments we identified in our sample; and, as appropriate, recovering any overpayments associated with nonsampled services; strengthening the physician education process; developing a data match that will identify physician services at high risk for place-of-service miscoding, and recovering any identified overpayments.

Medicare Claims for Home Blood-Glucose Test Strips and Lancets

In separate audits of three Medicare administrative contractors, HHS/OIG estimated that about $169.7 million could have been saved for CY 2007 had controls been in place to ensure that claims for blood-glucose test strips and/or lancets complied with certain Medicare documentation requirements. Medicare Part B covers test strips and lancets that physicians prescribe for diabetics. Medicare utilization guidelines allow up to 100 test strips and 100 lancets every month for insulin-treated diabetics and every three months for non-insulin-treated diabetics. Additional requirements apply for reimbursements of claims for quantities of test strips and lancets that exceed the utilization guidelines. HHS/OIG recommended, among other things, that the contractors implement system edits to identify high-utilization claims for test strips and/or lancets and work with CMS to develop cost-effective ways of determining which claims should be further reviewed for compliance with Medicare documentation requirements and enforce Medicare documentation requirements for claims for test strips and/or lancets.

Independent Diagnostic Testing Facilities' Compliance with Medicare Standards

HHS/OIG found in two studies that independent diagnostic testing facilities (IDTF) in the Miami and Los Angeles areas did not comply with Medicare's requirement that they maintain their physical facilities at the locations on file with CMS and be open during business hours. IDTFs that do not comply with Medicare standards are subject to administrative actions, including revocation of their Medicare billing privileges. In prior site visits in 1997, OIG found that 20 percent of IDTFs were not at the locations on file with CMS. HHS/OIG recommended, among other things, that CMS periodically conduct unannounced visits on IDTFs and that it impose a moratorium on the new enrollment of IDTFs in the Los Angeles area.

Medicare Payments for Outpatient Services

In seven reviews of each of seven Medicare contractors, HHS/OIG found that they made incorrect Medicare payments to hospitals in excess of their charges for outpatient services for four-year audit periods. Together, the incorrect payments included an estimated $37.9 million and involved excessive units of service, HCPCS codes that did not reflect the procedures performed, unallowable services, and lack of supporting documentation. HHS/OIG recommended that the contractors recover the unallowable amounts in identified overpayments and use the results of this audit in its hospital education activities.

HHS/OIG found that Medicare's per-beneficiary spending on outpatient therapy services in Florida's Miami-Dade County was three times the national average in 2009. HHS/OIG identified 20 high-utilization counties that had, in 2009, the highest average Medicare payment per beneficiary and more than $1 million in total Medicare payments for outpatient therapy. HHS/OIG analyzed Miami-Dade County separately from the other 19 counties because it had the highest average Medicare payments per beneficiary among the high-utilization counties and the highest total Medicare payments for outpatient therapy in 2009. Medicare's per-beneficiary spending on outpatient therapy services in the 19 other high-utilization counties as a group was 72 percent greater than the national average. HHS/OIG found that for five of six questionable billing characteristics that may indicate fraud, Miami-Dade's levels were at least three times the national levels. The other 19 counties also exhibited questionable billing. As a group, the other 19 counties had at least twice the national levels for five of the six questionable billing characteristics. HHS/OIG recommended, among other things, that CMS target outpatient therapy claims in high-utilization areas for further review and target outpatient therapy claims with questionable billing characteristics for further review.

Ambulatory Surgical Center Services Provided During Part A Skilled Nursing Facility Stays

Based on our sample results, HHS/OIG found that Medicare contractors made at least an estimated $6.6 million in overpayments to ambulatory surgical centers for services provided to beneficiaries during Part A skilled nursing facility (SNF) stays in CYs 2006 through 2008. All 100 services that HHS/OIG reviewed were already included in the SNFs' Part A payments but were nevertheless billed to Medicare Part B. As a result, Medicare paid twice for these services. HHS/OIG recommended, among other things, that CMS instruct its Medicare contractors to recover the $103,000 in overpayments for the 100 incorrectly billed services in our sample and review the 20,806 services that HHS/OIG did not review and recover overpayments estimated to total at least $6.5 million.

Medicare Payments for Ultra-High Therapy at Skilled Nursing Facilities

HHS/OIG found that from 2006 to 2008, SNFs increasingly billed for higher-paying resource utilization groups, even though beneficiary characteristics remained largely unchanged. In that period, Medicare payments to SNFs for ultra-high therapy increased by nearly 90 percent, rising from $5.7 billion to $10.7 billion. For billing purposes, SNFs categorize Medicare beneficiaries into resource utilization groups (RUG) based on their care and resource needs at various points during their stays. The RUGs for ultra-high therapy apply to those beneficiaries needing higher levels of therapy, and for which Medicare generally pays more. This review raised concerns about the potentially inappropriate use of higher-paying RUGs, particularly those for ultra-high therapy. HHS/OIG recommended, among other things, that CMS monitor overall payments to SNFs and adjust rates, if necessary, and change the current method for determining how much therapy is needed to ensure appropriate payments.

Employment of Individuals with Criminal Records at Medicare Skilled Nursing Facilities

HHS/OIG found that almost all (92 percent) of the nursing facilities in its review employed at least one individual with at least one criminal conviction. HHS/OIG analyzed criminal history records maintained by the FBI and found that overall, five percent of nursing facility employees had at least one criminal conviction. Forty-four percent of employees with criminal convictions committed crimes against property such as burglary, shoplifting, and writing bad checks. Most convictions occurred prior to employment. HHS/OIG also found that the FBI's records do not contain information on whether the victim of a crime was a nursing facility resident and the records therefore cannot be used by themselves to determine whether a conviction disqualifies an individual from nursing facility employment. HHS/OIG recommended that CMS develop background check procedures, including clearly defining the employee classifications that are direct patient access employees and working with participating states to develop a list of convictions that disqualify an individual from nursing facility employment under federal regulation and timeframes in which each conviction bars the individual from employment.

Medicare Hospices and Nursing Facility Residents

HHS/OIG found that Medicare spending on hospice care for nursing facility residents has grown nearly 70 percent since 2005 and that hundreds of hospices, most of which were for profit, had more than two-thirds of their beneficiaries in nursing facilities in 2009. Hospices with a high percentage of their beneficiaries in nursing homes received more Medicare payments per beneficiary than other hospices and had beneficiaries who spent more time in care. The high-percentage hospices typically enrolled beneficiaries whose diagnoses required less complex care and who already lived in nursing facilities. HHS/OIG recommended that CMS monitor hospices that depend heavily on nursing facility residents and modify the payment system for hospice care in nursing facilities. The current payment structure provides incentives for hospices to seek out nursing facility beneficiaries who often receive longer but less complex care. Medicare currently pays hospices the same rate for care provided in nursing facilities as it does for care provided in other settings, such as private homes. However, unlike private homes, nursing facilities (which are often paid by third-party payers or Medicaid) are already staffed with professional caregivers and are required to provide personal care services that are similar to hospice aide services.

Surety Bonds for Medicare Durable Medical Equipment

HHS/OIG's review revealed that Medicare had not recovered any DME overpayments through surety bonds. More than two years after publishing a January 2009 final rule requiring certain suppliers of durable medical equipment, prosthetics, orthotics, and supplies (DMEPOS) to obtain surety bonds, CMS had not finalized procedures for recovering overpayments through such bonds. The Balanced Budget Act of 1997 mandated that all nonexempt DMEPOS suppliers obtain a surety bond of not less than $50,000 to receive Medicare billing privileges. Requiring surety bonds serves as a means for Medicare to guarantee recoupment of some overpayments. The report contained no recommendations.

Medically Unnecessary Medicare Durable Medical Equipment

HHS/OIG found that an estimated 61 percent of power wheelchairs provided to Medicare beneficiaries in the first half of 2007 were medically unnecessary or had claims that lacked sufficient documentation to determine medical necessity. The estimate was based on records submitted by suppliers that provided the power wheelchairs. HHS/OIG recommended that Medicare enhance reenrollment screening standards for current DMEPOS suppliers, review records from sources in addition to the supplier such as the prescribing physician to determine medical necessity, continue supplier and physician education, and review the suppliers of the sampled claims we found to be in error.

Preventing Improper Medicare Payments

Using the reported error rate data from the Hospital Payment Monitoring Program and the Comprehensive Error Rate Testing program for FYs 2005 through 2008, HHS/OIG identified 740 error-prone providers. These providers accounted for a significant portion of the total dollars in error in the sampled years. Focusing on error-prone providers for corrective action and repayment of improper payments could improve the effectiveness of CMS's efforts to reduce improper payments. HHS/OIG recommended, among other things, that CMS use available error rate data to identify error-prone providers and require error-prone providers to identify the root causes of claim errors and to develop and implement corrective action plans.

HHS/OIG found that CMS used payment suspensions in 2007 and 2008 almost exclusively as a tool to fight fraud, though the sanction is available in overpayment circumstances short of fraud, and that CMS's guidance on payment suspensions to its contractors has incomplete or inconsistent requirements. After HHS/OIG collected data for this evaluation, the ACA established new provisions for payment suspensions. The ACA states that a provider's payments may be suspended based on a credible allegation of fraud, unless there is good cause not to suspend such payments. The statute also requires CMS to consult with OIG in determining whether a credible allegation of fraud exists. CMS published final regulations implementing these provisions in February 2011.

Medicare Payments for Brand-Name Inhalation Drugs

HHS/OIG found that Medicare payments to South Florida suppliers for the inhalation drug budesonide were reduced by almost half after Medicare implemented a utilization edit for the drug in September 2008. However, the decreases were offset by payments for the inhalation drug arformoterol (for which there was no edit), which then more than doubled within six months. Medicare paid South Florida suppliers for up to 10 times more units of arformoterol than were distributed for sale in the geographic area. The substantial difference between the sales data provided by arformoterol's manufacturer and the claims data for South Florida suppliers suggests that these suppliers were billing for drugs that may not have been actually purchased. HHS/OIG recommended that CMS require DME contractors to implement utilization edits in high-fraud areas as soon as Medicare begins paying for a brand-name drug, monitor utilization changes among brand-name inhalation drugs, strengthen initial claim review processes to focus on prevention of improper payments, and perform site visits and request documentation to support budesonide and arformoterol billings from the South Florida suppliers that HHS/OIG will refer for further review.

Medicare Claims for Atypical Antipsychotic Drugs

HHS/OIG found that for the period January 1 through June 30, 2007, 51 percent of Medicare claims for atypical antipsychotic drugs did not comply with Medicare reimbursement criteria, amounting to about $116 million in erroneous payments. Atypical antipsychotic drugs are approved by the FDA for treatment of schizophrenia and/or bipolar disorder. Recommendations included facilitating Medicare's access to information necessary to ensure accurate coverage and reimbursement determinations and taking appropriate action regarding the erroneous payments identified in our sample.

HHS/OIG's review did not evaluate the medical decisions used to determine each resident's treatment.

Medicare Payment for Drug Treatments for Age-Related Macular Degenerations

HHS/OIG found that if Medicare reimbursement for all beneficiaries treated with Avastin or Lucentis for wet age-related macular degeneration (wet AMD) had been paid at the Avastin rate during CYs 2008 and 2009, Medicare Part B would have saved approximately $1.1 billion and beneficiaries would have saved approximately $275 million in copayments. Our recommendations included evaluating coverage and reimbursement policies and seeking such additional authorities as are necessary to limit Part B drug and biological expenditures effectively. Avastin and Lucentis (both manufactured by Genentech) are the most commonly administered Part B biologicals used to treat wet AMD, which is the leading cause of severe vision loss in people over the age of 65 in the United States.

Terminated Drugs in Medicare Part D

Of the approximately $115 billion in gross drug costs included in Medicare Part D sponsors' prescription drug event (PDE) data for CYs 2006 and 2007, HHS/OIG found that CMS accepted PDE data totaling $112.1 million associated with 2,967 terminated drugs. CMS uses final PDE data to reconcile prospective payments made to Part D sponsors with actual costs. Terminated drugs are discontinued drugs that have passed their shelf life or drugs that have been pulled from the market for health or safety reasons. Such medications could be weak, ineffective, or detrimental to beneficiaries' health. However, federal regulations do not specifically prohibit coverage of terminated drugs under the Part D program. HHS/OIG recommended that CMS issue regulations to prohibit Medicare Part D coverage of terminated drugs and, in the interim, publish a list of these drugs on its Web site.

Erectile Dysfunction Drugs in the Medicare Part D Program

Of approximately $133 billion in gross drug costs included in private prescription drug plans' and MA plans' (collectively known as sponsors) PDE data for CYs 2007 and 2008, HHS/OIG found that CMS improperly accepted PDE data totaling $3.1 million in gross Medicare Part D drug costs for erectile dysfunction (ED) drugs approved only for the treatment of sexual or erectile dysfunction. Effective January 1, 2007, Part D should not have covered these drugs. HHS/OIG recommended that CMS determine whether it can impose financial adjustments on sponsors that were paid for furnishing ED drugs used for the treatment of sexual or erectile dysfunction and strengthen internal controls to help ensure that drugs covered by Medicare Part D comply with federal requirements by collaborating with FDA to create and maintain a comprehensive list of ED drugs that have been approved by FDA for the treatment of sexual or erectile dysfunction, regularly disseminating this list to all sponsors, and periodically updating the edit used to reject PDE data for ED drugs used for the treatment of sexual or erectile dysfunction.

Identifying Prescribers in Medicare Part D Drug Data

HHS/OIG's audit of PDE records for drugs classified as Schedule II pursuant to the Controlled Substances Act revealed approximately 228,000 PDE records with invalid prescriber identifiers, accounting for about $20.6 million in gross drug costs for CY 2007. Without valid identifiers from sponsors, CMS and its Part D contractors might not be able to monitor excessive prescribing patterns, determine whether a prescription was written by an excluded or deceased provider, or identify those physicians who illegally prescribe Schedule II drugs. Schedule II drugs have a high potential for abuse, have an accepted medical use with severe restrictions, and may cause severe psychological or physical dependence if abused. Because of invalid prescriber identifiers, HHS/OIG was unable to identify top prescribers for oxycodone, Ritalin, and methadone, which are three Schedule II drugs that are frequently involved in health care investigations. HHS/OIG recommended that CMS issue specific guidance requiring sponsors to include a valid DEA number on standard and nonstandard format PDE records involving Schedule II drugs and implement an edit to reject PDE records for Schedule II drugs when the prescriber identifier field contains an invalid prescriber identifier number.

Rebates in Medicare Part D

HHS/OIG found that Part D sponsors underestimated rebates in 69 percent of their bids for plan year 2008, which led to higher beneficiary premiums and caused both beneficiaries and the government to overpay for the benefit. Part D sponsors' bids to participate in Part D include estimates of the cost to provide the benefit to each beneficiary. CMS uses bids to calculate beneficiary premiums for each plan. Sponsors also negotiate drug manufacturer rebates and other price concessions to reduce the cost of the program to beneficiaries and the Federal government. Sponsors must include an estimate in their bids of the rebates they expect to receive for the plan year. Underestimating rebates increases beneficiary premiums. HHS/OIG also found that, although sponsors may pass rebates on to beneficiaries at the point of sale to reduce beneficiaries' drug costs and copayments, they commonly did not. HHS/OIG recommended, among other things, that CMS take steps to ensure that sponsors more accurately include their expected rebates in their bids.

Other Fraud and Abuse Prevention Activities

In addition to amounts specifically designated by statute for HHS/OIG activities, HHS/OIG was allocated $1.5 million in FY 2010 for Compliance Training and Data Mining Activities. These activities continued into FY 2011.

HHS/OIG's HEAT Provider Compliance Training initiative (HEAT PCT) provided free, high-quality compliance training for providers, compliance professionals, and attorneys in Strike Force cities and elsewhere. HEAT PCT, which included presenters from HHS/OIG, CMS Regional Offices, CMS Program Integrity, USAOs, and state Medicaid Fraud Control Units, held sessions in Houston, Tampa, Kansas City, Baton Rouge, Denver, and Washington, D.C., training a total of 737 in-person attendees. In addition, the final HEAT PCT session in Washington, D.C., was webcast live to 2,335 participants. HHS/OIG developed comprehensive training materials to accompany HEAT PCT, and those materials are now available online at no charge, together with sixteen video modules dividing the webcast by subject area that will continue reaching the health care community with our compliance message.

In FY 2011, HCFAC funding also supported HHS/OIG's continued enhancement of data analysis and mining capabilities for detecting health care fraud, including tools that allow for complex data analysis. OIG is using data mining, predictive analytics, trend evaluation, and modeling approaches to better analyze and target the oversight of HHS programs. Analysis teams use near-time data to examine Medicare claims for known fraud patterns, identify suspected fraud trends, and to calculate ratios of allowed services as compared with national averages, as well as other assessments. When united with the expertise of OIG agents, auditors, and evaluators, as well as our HEAT partners, HHS/OIG's data analysis fosters a highly effective combination of technologies and traditional skills to the fight against fraud, waste, and abuse.

OIG also proposed providing MFCUs greater flexibility to conduct their own data mining activities. On March 17, 2011, OIG issued a Notice of Proposed Rulemaking, 76 Fed. Reg. 14637, that would amend a provision in HHS regulations that prohibits MFCUs from using federal matching funds to identify fraud through screening and analysis of state Medicaid claims data, known as data mining. The provision, contained in 42 CFR § 1007.19, would be amended to permit federal matching for data mining when MFCUs meet certain conditions. Comments on the proposal were due on May 16, 2011.

Industry Outreach and Guidance

Advisory Opinions

Central to the HIPAA guidance initiatives is an advisory opinion process through which parties may obtain binding legal guidance as to whether their existing or proposed health care business transactions run afoul of the AKS, the CMP laws, or the exclusion provisions. During FY 2011, the HHS/OIG, in consultation with DOJ, issued 22 advisory opinions. A total of 255 advisory opinions have been issued during the 15 years of the HCFAC program.

Corporate and Other Integrity Agreements

Many health care providers that enter agreements with the government to settle potential liabilities for violations of the FCA also agree to adhere to a separate CIA, Integrity Agreement, or other similar agreement. Under these agreements, the provider commits to establishing a program or taking other specified steps to ensure its future compliance with Medicare and Medicaid rules. At the close of FY 2011, HHS/OIG was monitoring compliance with 245 such agreements.

Centers for Medicare & Medicaid Services

In FY 2011, CMS was allocated approximately $22.3 million by HHS, and appropriated $250.9 million in discretionary funds by Congress to support a variety of projects related to fraud, waste, and abuse in the Medicare and Medicaid programs and the Children's Health Insurance Program (CHIP). With these funds, CMS has continued to build on existing fraud prevention activities and implement new advanced technology to ensure that accurate payments are made to legitimate providers for appropriate and reasonable services for eligible beneficiaries of the federal health care programs. It is important to note that CMS is engaged in many program integrity activities that are beyond the scope of this report because they are not funded directly by the HCFAC Account or discretionary HCFAC funding. For example, Medicare Integrity Program (MIP) activities, such as audit and medical review functions, Medicare Fee-for-Service error rate measurement, and Medicaid Integrity program activities are discussed in separate reports.

CMS has taken four major approaches to fraud prevention and organizing its key anti-fraud, waste, and abuse activities:

1. Prevention
2. Detection
3. Transparency and Accountability
4. Recovery

1. Prevention

The Affordable Care Act (ACA)

The new authorities granted to HHS and CMS under ACA have been instrumental in further clamping down on fraudulent activity in the health care sector. In FY 2011, CMS implemented ACA authorities to keep out fraudulent providers and suppliers. CMS published the Final Rule with comment entitled "Medicare, Medicaid, and Children's Health Insurance Programs; Additional Screening Requirements, Application Fees, Temporary Enrollment Moratoria, Payment Suspensions and Compliance Plans for Providers and Suppliers" (CMS-6028-FC) on February 2, 2011 and it has been effective since March 25, 2011. First, this rule created a rigorous risk-based screening process for all new and re-enrolling providers and suppliers enrolling in Medicare, Medicaid, or CHIP. Under this rule, categories of providers and suppliers are assigned to one of three levels of screening based on their risk of fraud—limited, moderate, or high. Moderate and high risk providers are subject to announced and unannounced site visits. The regulation also imposed a requirement that high risk providers and suppliers undergo a fingerprint-based criminal background check. Second, this rule established a moratorium authority to allow CMS to temporarily halt the enrollment of specific categories of providers or suppliers when CMS determines there is a significant potential for fraud, waste, or abuse with respect to a particular provider or supplier type, a particular geographic area, or both. Third, this rule enabled CMS to suspend payments to a provider or supplier pending the investigation of a credible allegation of fraud. CMS believes that each of these provisions will greatly enhance its program integrity efforts.

National Fraud Prevention Program

CMS' National Fraud Prevention Program uses two concurrent approaches to fraud prevention in Medicare fee-for-service: predictive analytics for claims, which was implemented on June 30, 2011, and provider screening for enrollment, which will begin in FY 2012. By leveraging sophisticated analytic tools in claims processing and provider enrollment, CMS can better identify fraudulent claims and high-risk applicants, and take swift and appropriate action to protect the Trust Funds. CMS anticipates that its continued use and ongoing enhancement of sophisticated analytical technologies will enable it to better combat fraud, waste, and abuse in Medicare, Medicaid, and CHIP.

- *The Fraud Prevention System:* The Fraud Prevention System (FPS), CMS' new predictive modeling technology, was launched on June 30, 2011 pursuant to the Small Business Jobs Act of 2010. The FPS analyzes all Medicare fee-for-service claims using risk-based algorithms developed by CMS and the private sector, prior to payment, allowing CMS to take prompt action where appropriate. While the development of the FPS is not directly funded by HCFAC, many activities in this report support the FPS. Based on the predictive technologies used in the credit card industry, the FPS uses historical data and external databases to identify unusual patterns and determine the likelihood of fraudulent activity. The FPS has been streaming claims on a prepayment basis since June 30, 2011, enabling CMS and its investigative partners to stop payment of fraudulent claims and respond to emerging trends. CMS is exploring ways to apply predictive modeling technology to the Medicaid program.
- *SAS Statistical Programming License:* CMS established an analytics lab to develop and test new models for the FPS and secure licenses for SAS statistical programming software to analyze claims data to identify aberrant billing patterns and program vulnerabilities. As of the end of FY 2011, CMS has added nine new models to the FPS, and nine additional models were under active development for future integration in the FPS. Going forward, CMS will develop models on a continuous basis.
- *One Program Integrity:* In FY 2011, CMS continued to make enhancements, perform maintenance, and upgrade analytic tools. The One Program Integrity (One PI) data project provides a fully integrated searchable database of all Medicare paid claims and is used to perform data analysis across the centralized Integrated Data Repository (IDR). The IDR contains a comprehensive and accurate set of Medicare provider, beneficiary and claims data for Medicare Parts A, B, and D back to January 2006. One PI improves CMS' ability to detect fraud, waste, and abuse with consistent, reliable, and timely analyses.

CMS has expanded the data repository in order to accommodate the increasing volume of data. CMS added additional data streams and reference data to the IDR and began data analysis on an approach for standardized Medicaid data. CMS is continuing its participation in a ten state pilot to explore innovative technologies and methodologies for transforming, loading, and analyzing this data.

CMS also continued to train law enforcement on the use of the Medicare analytic tools and data systems. In FY 2011, CMS doubled the number of training courses available and significantly restructured the training courses to give users more hands-on instruction.

- *Provider Enrollment Screening:* To strengthen and help implement the new provider enrollment requirements under the ACA, CMS awarded a contract for Automated Provider Screening (APS) and began implementing the process in FY 2011 to verify Provider Enrollment, Chain and Ownership System (PECOS) enrollment data for CMS' fee-for-service providers and suppliers. The APS will evaluate enrollment applications against known indicators of fraud; provide access to a rich set of screened data results; be accessible through a secure browser user interface; and allow for integration with CMS systems. This new process will launch in early 2012 and permit CMS to quickly identify ineligible, and potentially fraudulent, enrollment applications. The integration of this automated provider screening tool with the enrollment data in the Provider, Enrollment, Chain and Ownership System and the claims data in the Fraud Prevention System (FPS) will improve CMS' ability to screen and identify questionable entities more efficiently, which will lead to cost-avoidance and increased savings for Medicare.
- *Provider Screening Lab:* CMS has worked with Mitre, a Federally Funded Research and Development Center (FFRDC), to establish the Mitre Provider Screening Lab. The provider screening lab tests proof of concepts for new provider screening data sources, methodologies, and associated algorithms. To date, the lab has provided effective provider screening by utilizing a variety of data sets, including PECOS, the Compromised Numbers Checklist (CNC), and HHS/OIG's Medicare Exclusion Database, to name a few. Additional data sources will be evaluated in the future.

Compromised Number Checklist (CNC)

In January 2010, CMS released its first national database of compromised Medicare beneficiary and provider ID numbers called the Compromised Number Checklist (CNC). This database is populated by monthly submissions from program integrity contractors. The purpose of the CNC is to share compromised ID numbers and any associated corrective actions that have been taken. CMS continues to leverage this national CNC database to enhance efforts detecting and preventing fraud and abuse in Medicare.

The compromised numbers are updated on a monthly basis. In 2011, the CNC identified approximately 5,000 compromised providers and suppliers and approximately 280,000 beneficiaries whose Health Insurance Claim Number (HICN) is known or strongly suspected to have been compromised. The CNC also utilizes geomapping analyses to identify "clustering" of compromised numbers, which is extremely valuable in the development of new investigations.

Medicare Beneficiary Compromised Number Checklist Verification Pilot

In FY 2011, CMS began testing a methodology to identify the reasons why beneficiary HICNs appear in the CNC. For the pilot, CMS will contact beneficiaries by letter to determine if their HICNs can be validated as compromised. Once verified, the HICNs will be incorporated into the FPS to identify schemes or patterns indicative of fraud.

Next Generation Desktop

CMS began implementation of an enhanced Next Generation Desktop on September 10, 2011. CMS collaborated with National Government Services (NGS), a Medicare Administrative Contractor (MAC), to respond to requests from law enforcement for enhanced views of provider data, including the ability to drill down into actual fraud complaints against the provider and display claims associated with a provider tax ID. CMS and NGS developed tailored training material for law enforcement partners and will provide training classes to law enforcement staff three times a year. CMS anticipates training up to 75 individuals in FY 2012.

DMEPOS Competitive Bidding and other DME Initiatives

CMS has undertaken numerous aggressive actions to address program integrity concerns with DMEPOS suppliers with a comprehensive strategy:

- *DMEPOS Competitive Bidding:* The DMEPOS Competitive Bidding Program strengthens Medicare by taking an important step towards paying appropriately for medical equipment and supplies. Competitive bidding reduces out-of-pocket costs for consumers and is estimated to save the Medicare program billions over 10 years. All suppliers in the competitive bidding program must be licensed, meet strict quality and financial standards, and be accredited by a national accreditation organization. Importantly, DMEPOS competitive bidding helps to prevent Medicare fraud because reduction in excessive payment amounts makes competitively bid items less attractive targets for fraud and abuse. In addition, suppliers are subject to stricter standards in order to participate in the Competitive Bidding program, therefore keeping fraudulent suppliers at bay from Medicare.

  As of January 1, 2011, CMS' DMEPOS Competitive Bidding Program Round 1 Rebid has occurred in the following nine Metropolitan Statistical Areas (MSAs):

  - Cincinnati–Middletown (Ohio, Kentucky and Indiana)
  - Cleveland–Elyria–Mentor (Ohio)
  - Charlotte–Gastonia-Concord (North Carolina and South Carolina)
  - Dallas–Fort Worth–Arlington (Texas)
  - Kansas City (Missouri and Kansas)
  - Miami–Fort Lauderdale – Pompano Beach (Florida)
  - Orlando – Kissimmee (Florida)
  - Pittsburgh (Pennsylvania)
  - Riverside–San Bernardino – Ontario (California)

- *DMEPOS Surety Bond:* Since 2009, CMS has made it a requirement for DMEPOS suppliers to post surety bonds prior to enrollment. CMS also implemented DMEPOS Accreditation Standards which have been in effect since October 1, 2009. Supplier numbers cannot be issued or renewed unless the supplier - assuming it does not otherwise qualify for an exception under 42 CFR § 424.57(d)(15) - obtains and maintains a surety bond of at least $50,000 and meets the accreditation standards on a continuous basis.
- *DMEPOS Swipe Card Pilot:* The DMEPOS Swipe Card Pilot was designed to test strategies for implementation of section 6406 of the

Affordable Care Act, which requires that physicians and other suppliers maintain, and provide upon request, DMEPOS ordering and referring information. Beginning in FY 2011, physicians and other participating suppliers swipe magnetic cards (similar to credit cards) and enter a code into existing credit card terminals when placing or filling DMEPOS orders. CMS, through a contract with National Government Services (NGS), uses this information to confirm that the orders were appropriately initiated and filled.

Through FY 2011, over 9,600 swipe cards and informational materials were distributed to the providers and suppliers in the Indianapolis area. Provider outreach was conducted by using multiple venues and media formats (list-serve electronic notices, conferences, direct provider outreach using traditional mail, cold calling and personal visits). Because participation in the pilot is voluntary, CMS is closely monitoring provider and supplier participation levels.

Fraud Prevention Campaign

In FY 2011, CMS continued to work with the Assistant Secretary for Public Affairs (ASPA) to build on the Fraud Prevention Campaign to increase public awareness about Medicare's fight against fraud. The project was launched in January 2010, and FY 2011 work was supported with FY 2010 HCFAC dollars. HCFAC funding received in FY 2011 will be used in FY 2012 to continue outreach tactics to inform Medicare beneficiaries how to prevent, detect, and report Medicare fraud. Findings from this outreach will be reported in the FY 2012 HCFAC report. Additional information on the Fraud Prevention Campaign is included in the ASPA section of this report.

2. Detection

Strengthened Program Integrity Activities in Medicare Advantage and Medicare Part D

In FY 2011, CMS established a contract for Medicare Advantage (Part C) and Medicare Prescription Drug (Part D) outreach and education. This contractor is responsible for coordinating all Part C and Part D program integrity outreach activities for all stakeholders, including plan sponsors and law enforcement. This contractor also supports compliance audits and fraud audits. Additionally, CMS continued to fund the Program Integrity Technical Assistance contractor to support Part C and Part D program integrity strategy, ROI methodology, performance measure database maintenance, development of program risk assessment processes, and other technical assistance as requested. CMS also contracted with the Compliance and Enforcement Medicare Drug Integrity Contractor (MEDIC) to conduct ad-hoc studies and analysis with a special focus on select geographic areas.

Additionally, CMS continued to invest HCFAC discretionary funds to strengthen Medicare Part C and Part D oversight. CMS contracts with the MEDICs for all Medicare Advantage and Part D program integrity work, including:

- Managing all incoming complaints about Part C and Part D fraud, waste, and abuse;
- Utilizing new and innovative techniques to monitor and analyze information to help identify potential fraud;
- Working with law enforcement, MA, and prescription drug plans, consumer groups, and other key partners to protect consumers and enforce Medicare's rules;
- Providing basic tips for consumers on how to protect themselves from potential scams;
- Identifying program vulnerabilities; and
- Performing proactive research utilizing all available data to find trends in order to ferret out fraud, waste, and abuse activities.

In FY 2011, the national benefit integrity MEDIC received approximately 342 actionable complaints (within the MEDIC's scope) per month; processed 34 requests for information from law enforcement per month; and referred an average of 36 cases per month. The national benefit integrity MEDIC was responsible for assisting HHS/OIG and DOJ (through data analysis and investigative case development) in achieving four guilty pleas, seven arrests, and eight indictments. One case produced a 34-count indictment and included a group of 25 individuals and 26 pharmacies owned by one individual in the Detroit area involving approximately $38 million in Medicare funds. The national benefit integrity MEDIC has also been a key participant in investigating a Part D drug scheme that originated in West Hollywood, California. Many case referrals have resulted from this project and formed the basis for multiple future indictments.

In addition to the work of the MEDICs, CMS enhanced other Part C and Part D oversight functions in FY 2011 to address new complexities facing law enforcement; contract and plan oversight functions; monitor plan performance assessment and surveillance/secret shopper activities; audit programs; and conduct routine compliance and enforcement tracking. In FY 2011, CMS conducted 11 program audits of sponsoring organizations and tested for compliance with program requirements relating to Part D formulary and benefit administration, Part D coverage determinations, appeals and grievances, independent agent and broker oversight, and compliance program effectiveness. These audits covered programs that accounted for 25 percent of all MA and Prescription Drug Plan contracts and 42 percent of all beneficiaries enrolled as of May 2011. Additionally, in FY 2011 CMS issued more than 1,300 compliance actions to Part C and Part D sponsors covering a wide range of topics, such as benefit administration, bid submission, call letter requirements, claims processing, formulary administration, low income subsidy administration, and payment concerns.

CMS also strengthened program integrity in MA and Part D through marketing surveillance activities and compliance actions based on surveillance activities:

- *Marketing Surveillance Activities:* In FY 2011, CMS conducted many marketing surveillance activities, such as secret shopping and examining newspaper ads for unreported marketing events and content. These activities have improved plan sponsor oversight of marketing activities and lessened incidents of agent/broker marketplace misconduct.

  For the 2011 Annual Enrollment Period (AEP), CMS conducted 1,938 secret shopping events, a record number, and an increase of 125.9 percent from the 2010 AEP. Secret shopping is the undercover surveillance of formal, public MA and Part D plan marketing events to ensure agents and brokers are providing accurate information to Medicare beneficiaries and are in compliance with our marketing rules for Parts C and D. CMS believes that its significant outreach efforts helped decrease deficiencies for formal marketing events. The number of "absolute statements" (such as "we are the best" or "we are number one") made about MA and Part D decreased from 54 instances during the 2010 AEP season to 32 instances during the 2011 AEP season. In addition, the number of events that were reported to CMS that did not take place decreased from 115 during the 2010 AEP season to 53 during the 2011 AEP season. AEP data for 2011 demonstrated that the communication efforts were effective and the message was well received by plan sponsors and other external stakeholders.

Targeted Observations

During the 2011 AEP, the Targeted Observation (TO) initiative captured observations of alleged marketing misrepresentation by agents or brokers in settings outside of formal sales presentations. CMS created this surveillance activity following concerns about plan sponsors approaching beneficiaries outside of retail stores, misrepresenting products at informal informational tables, and other conduct that would not be captured through CMS' previous surveillance strategy. TOs were conducted based on information received from internal and external partners. CMS performed 31 TOs on 11 plan sponsors, and performed four TOs not attributed to any particular plan sponsor. The TOs were prompted by alleged agent misbehavior at various settings, including kiosks in megastores and door-to-door solicitations. Other TOs investigated unsolicited phone calls and the use of lead generator websites that appeared to be endorsed by CMS.

Plan sponsors reviewed the results and took appropriate action ranging from training to terminating agents. Without specific direction from CMS, plan sponsors may use the information found through the TO process to make a determination to take action against a particular agent. Specifically, two plan sponsors each voluntarily terminated an agent for engaging in egregious marketing activities. One agent was using "scare tactics" by stating that beneficiaries could only receive their prescription drugs through the specific retail store's pharmacy. The agent utilized superlatives in describing the plan sponsor's products, stated that Medicare was going away, and told the beneficiaries that they needed to sign up for his plan or they would not have any drug coverage next year. CMS believes that expanding the use of TOs will provide additional opportunities to monitor agents and brokers in settings outside of formal sales presentations to determine if violations occur during non-formal public encounters.

Unreported Marketing Events

The unreported marketing events initiative was an effort to determine if plan sponsors were appropriately reporting and representing their sales events activity to CMS. The CMS contractor reviewed daily and weekly print publications in U.S. domestic markets nationwide, including advertisements in publications in English, Spanish, Korean, Armenian, and Mandarin Chinese. The contractor then determined if event information identified in the "clipped" advertisements was properly reported to CMS in a timely manner.

Under CMS' direction, a surveillance contractor reviewed advertisements that accounted for 5,256 unique events from October to December 2010. The advertisements reviewed encompassed a total of 75 plan sponsors, of which 57 submitted 100 percent of the clipped marketing events to HPMS in an accurate and timely manner. The remaining 18 plan sponsors had one or more deficiencies, with a total of 232 deficiencies identified.

- Compliance Actions Based on Surveillance Activities: In order of severity, potential compliance actions consist of Technical Assistance Letters (informal compliance actions), Notices of Non-Compliance, Warning Letters with a Request for Business Plan, and Ad-hoc Corrective Action Plans (CAPs). Listed below are the compliance actions taken for each primary surveillance activity.

Compliance Actions

Compliance Action	Secret Shopping Events	Unreported Marketing Events
Technical Assistance Letter*	102	17
Notice of Non-compliance	18	1
Warning Letter with Business Plan	4	0
Ad-hoc CAP	0	0
Total Letters Issued	124	18

*Technical Assistance Letters were sent to plan sponsors that were shopped, but either did not meet the minimum number of shops, no matter how many deficiencies were found, or had minimal findings.

For non-marketing related issues uncovered during a TO, CMS referred these issues to appropriate entities, including state Departments of Insurance and CMS Account Managers. In addition, CMS referred issues to the MEDIC responsible for investigating potential fraud, waste, and abuse in the Part C and Part D programs.

Medicaid/CHIP Financial Management Project

Under this project, funding specialists, including accountants and financial analysts, worked to improve CMS's financial oversight of the Medicaid program and CHIP. In FY 2011, through the continued efforts of these specialists, CMS removed an estimated $949 million (with approximately $915 million recovered and $34 million resolved) of approximately $6.3 billion identified in questionable Medicaid costs.

Furthermore, an estimated $223 million in questionable reimbursement was actually averted due to the funding specialists' preventive work with states to promote proper state Medicaid financing. The funding specialists' activities included reviews of proposed Medicaid state plan amendments that related to reimbursement; development of financial management reviews; research regarding state Medicaid financing policy and practices; collaboration with states to resolve the Medicaid and CHIP portions of the A-133 "Single State" audits; and identification of sources of the non-Federal share of Medicaid program payments to ensure proper financing of Medicaid program costs.

HHS/OIG Hotline Database

In FY 2011, CMS took strides toward the complete automation of the database to which HHS/OIG forwards some complaints received on the HHS/OIG Hotline. CMS also began incorporating HHS/OIG Hotline referrals and supporting documentation into the 1-800-Medicare fraud complaint workflow and system to foster consistency in CMS's handling of complaints and provide improved ability to track the lifecycle of the complaints; CMS and HHS/OIG anticipate implementing the new process by mid-2012.

3. Transparency and Accountability

Measured Error Rate - Payment Error Rate Measurement (PERM)

The Improper Payments Information Act (IPIA) of 2002, amended by the Improper Payments Elimination and Recovery Act of 2010 (IPERA), requires each agency to: periodically review programs it administers, identify programs that may be susceptible to significant improper payments, estimate the amount of improper payments, submit those estimates to Congress, and report on actions the Agency is taking to reduce improper payments. The Medicaid program and CHIP are identified as at risk for significant erroneous payments. To comply with the IPIA and IPERA, CMS established the Payment Error Rate Measurement (PERM) to estimate improper payment error rates in Medicaid and CHIP. The error rates are based on reviews of the fee-forservice (FFS), managed care, and eligibility components of Medicaid and CHIP in the fiscal year under review. CMS uses federal contractors to measure Medicaid and CHIP error rates using a 17-state rotation so that each state is reviewed once every three years. In 2006, CMS first measured the fee-for-service component of Medicaid. Starting in 2007, PERM was expanded to measure error rates for fee-for-service, managed care, and eligibility in both Medicaid and CHIP.

HHS calculated, and is reporting in the FY 2011 Agency Financial Report, the three-year weighted average national Medicaid error rate that includes the rates from fiscal years 2009, 2010, and 2011. This three-year rolling national error rate is 8.1 percent or $21.9 billion in estimated improper payments and has decreased from FY 2010 (9.4 percent). The weighted national error components rates are as follows: Medicaid FFS, 2.7 percent; Medicaid managed care, 0.3 percent; and Medicaid eligibility, 6.1 percent. The most common cause of errors in fee-forservice claims is lack of sufficient documentation to support the payment. The vast majority of the eligibility errors were due to beneficiaries found to be ineligible or whose eligibility status could not be determined.

In addition to differences in state programs, CMS notes that some of the agency's initial methodologies for classifying errors in PERM, particularly with respect to eligibility, drew criticism from states and other stakeholders resulting in Congressional action to revise the approach for future years. Congress included in the Children's Health Insurance Program Reauthorization Act of 2009 (CHIPRA) a provision stating that the payment error rate determined for a state should exclude certain payment errors as long as the state's process for verifying an applicant's self-declaration or self-certification of income was approved by CMS.

On August 11, 2010, CMS published a final PERM regulation allowing a self-declaration statement that is present in the case record to be used to verify eligibility for the PERM reviews if it meets certain requirements, such as not being out-of-date. If it does not meet these requirements, states may obtain a new self-declaration statement or verify the applicant's eligibility using third party sources, such as applicable caseworker notes or information obtained by the PERM reviewer. This provision conforms error rate measurement to Federal and state policies concerning eligibility process and required verifications. This revised eligibility review process is reflected in the Medicaid 2011 error rate and will be used in future Medicaid and CHIP error rates. Section 601 of CHIPRA prohibited HHS from calculating or publishing any national or state-specific error rates for CHIP until six months after the new PERM final rule was effective so HHS began CHIP error rate measurement in 2011 and will publish the results in November 2012.

CMS is currently measuring cycles that will be reported in 2012 and 2013. CMS expects the error rates for Medicaid to decline in future years through program maturation and corrective action initiatives implemented at the state and Federal levels. Additionally, in response to an HHS/OIG review of the FY 2008 PERM program described in the HHS/OIG section of this report, CMS formed a State Systems Workgroup to promote collaboration between CMS and states. CMS implemented a two-stage reconciliation process beginning with the FY 2009 PERM cycle to ensure that states' PERM universes are complete and accurate.

As a result of the President's Executive Order on Reducing Improper Payments, the PERM program has added several new requirements including reporting on the Treasury payment accuracy website and reporting comprehensive improper payment measurement and reduction activities to HHS/OIG.

Medicare Fee-for-Service (FFS) Error Rate Measurement

The FY 2011 Medicare FFS improper payment rate was 8.6 percent. While CMS continued to review claims according to a significantly revised and improved methodology, as implemented in FY 2009 in consultation with the HHS/OIG, the methodology was further refined in FY 2011 to reflect the impact that late documentation and the results of appeals activities have on the improper payment rate. The unadjusted rate (before factoring in appeals and receipt of additional documentation) for 2011 was 9.9 percent. The adjusted error rate more accurately reflects the estimated improper payment rate for the Medicare FFS program. Medicare Integrity Program (MIP) activities, such as measurement of the Medicare FFS error rate and medical review, are discussed further in a separate report.

Error Rate Measurement and Increased Accountability in Medicare Advantage (Part C) and Medicare Part D

In compliance with IPERA, CMS has prepared and implemented a systematic plan regarding improper payments for Part C and Part D programs. Unlike Medicare fee-for-service, CMS makes prospective, monthly per-capita payments to Part C organizations and Part D plan sponsors. Each per-person payment is based on a bid amount, approved by CMS, that reflects the plan's estimate of average costs to provide benefit coverage to enrollees. CMS risk-adjusts these payments to take into account the cost associated with treating individual beneficiaries based on health status. In addition, certain Part D prospective payments are reconciled against actual costs, and risk-sharing rules set in law are applied to further mitigate plan risk.

The Part C payment error estimate reported for FY 2011 (based on payment year 2009) is 11.0 percent, or $12.4 billion. This is a reduction from the FY 2010 payment error estimate of 14.1 percent. This reduction to 11.0 percent meets and exceeds the target error rate established for FY 2011 in the

FY 2010 Agency Financial Report. The FY 2011 Part C payment error estimate presents the combined impact on Part C payments of two sources of error: Part C payment system error and the Risk Adjustment Error. Most of the Part C payment error is driven by errors in risk adjustment data (clinical diagnosis data) submitted by Part C plans to CMS for payment purposes. Specifically, the Risk Adjustment Error estimate reflects the extent to which diagnoses that plans report to CMS are not supported by medical record documentation. The improvement in the Part C error rate can be attributed to the Administration's emphasis on contract-specific Risk Adjustment Data Validation (RADV) audits designed to recover overpayments to Part C plans, and to outreach and education to plans. Further, CMS has initiated outreach and education efforts for physicians/providers for FY 2012.

CMS conducts contract-specific RADV audits for the purpose of estimating risk adjustment error specific to Part C organizations. The RADV audits have created a sentinel effect in the industry. Part C organizations are more aware of the importance of properly documenting the clinical diagnoses they submit to CMS that can lead to enhanced Medicare payments. Further, Part C organizations are now aware that failure to have proper documentation will result in CMS' identification of overpayments for payment recovery purposes.

CMS is reporting for the first time a payment error estimate for the Part D program. The Part D payment error estimate reported for FY 2011 (based on payment year 2009) is 3.2 percent, or $1.7 billion. The FY 2011 Part D error estimate presents the combined impact on Part D payments of five sources of error: Part D payment system error; payment error related to low income subsidy status; payment error related to incorrect Medicaid status; payment error related to prescription drug event data validation; and payment error related to direct and indirect remuneration. Most of the Part D payment error is driven by errors related to prescription drug event data validation (PEPV). The FY 2011 PEPV rate of 2.18 percent represents a decrease of approximately 10 percentage points from the FY 2010 PEPV rate of 12.7 percent. This decrease is due largely to the Administration's efforts to provide plans with additional guidance to improve their collection of prescription documentation from pharmacies.

Probable Fraud Measurement Pilot

While CMS calculates an improper payments error rates in Medicare and Medicaid as described above, there is no agreed-upon agency estimate of how much fraud is in the Medicare program. In collaboration with the HHS Office of the Assistant Secretary for Planning and Evaluation, CMS began developing the first nationally representative estimates of the extent of probable fraud in the Medicare fee-for-service program in FY 2011. Documenting the baseline amount of fraud in Medicare is of critical importance as it allows officials to evaluate the success of ongoing fraud prevention activities. This pilot project will estimate probable fraud in one service area to pilot test the measurement approach and calculate a service-specific estimate. This pilot is measuring "probable fraud" rather than "fraud" because fraud is a legal determination that CMS cannot make on its own. A review panel of experienced health care analysts, clinicians, policy experts, and fraud investigators will review all collected data and determine if there is sufficient evidence to warrant a referral to law enforcement. After the completion of this pilot, CMS will assess the value of expanding the measurement to other areas of the program.

Fraud Summits

On June 8, 2010 President Obama announced a nationwide series of regional fraud prevention summits as part of a multi-faceted effort to crack down on health care fraud. HHS has a strong commitment to partnering with the private sector to mutually learn from best practices. Summits were held on July 16, 2010, in Miami; on August 26, 2010, in Los Angeles; on November 5, 2010, in Brooklyn; on December 16, 2010 in Boston; on March 15, 2011 in Detroit; and on June 17, 2011 in Philadelphia. FY 2010 HCFAC funds totaling $1 million were used to fund these regional fraud summits and also to underwrite the Fraud Prevention Campaign in both FY 2011 and FY 2012. More information on the fraud prevention summits is included in the ASPA section of this report.

4. Recovery

Field Offices

CMS has been placing resources in Medicare "hot fraud" areas with Zone Program Integrity Contractors (ZPIC) and CMS program integrity field offices. The ZPIC contracting strategy aligns the antifraud contractors with the MAC zones. Additionally, the designated program integrity field offices are located in or near the HEAT cites of Miami, Los Angeles, and Brooklyn, and provide an on the ground presence in high risk fraud areas of the country. Together, the field offices and ZPICs conduct data analysis to proactively identify targets and to coordinate efforts among various contractors and agencies to identify local issues and vulnerabilities with national or regional impact. All three field offices have staff that are designated CMS Strike Force Liaisons, who coordinate with law enforcement, facilitate data analysis, and expedite suspension requests.

Many special projects originate from the field offices that produce significant savings. These efforts have resulted in savings of $313.7 million and resulted in the revocation or deactivation of 883 provider numbers in FY 2011.

Enrollment Special Study

The Enrollment Special Study is a project designed to stop the fraudulent providers from obtaining new Medicare provider numbers, reduce the number of the habitual "bad providers" from re-entering the Medicare system after they have been kicked out, and shift from the pay and chase approach that has existed in years past. In this project, site visits are conducted prior to enrollment and providers are targeted for a closer review. The project is limited to Community Mental Health Centers (CMHCs), Comprehensive Outpatient Rehabilitation Facilities, and Independent Diagnostic Testing Facilities in South Florida. Once the MAC conducts a site visit, it assesses the provider's individual risk. If the provider appears to be suspect or pose an elevated risk of fraud, the provider is referred to the ZPIC for investigation and administrative action, as appropriate. This project began as a one year project in July 2009 and has been extended due to its success.

As of August 30, 2011, First Coast Service Operations, Inc. (FCSO), a MAC, has conducted over 11,795 activity checks to verify providers and suppliers' operational status, deactivated 430 providers, and revoked 410 providers. Since inception, FCSO saved $30.9 million from prepayment review and requested over $156,726 in overpayments. In addition, SafeGuard Services (SGS), the ZPIC, conducted over 1,050 on-site investigations resulting in 492 providers being revoked or deactivated. SGS placed 480 providers on prepayment review saving $15.3 million and requested $168.5 million in overpayments. To date, the project has resulted in $46.2 million in savings, with $24.3 million resulting in activity in the past year.

Florida Infusion Therapy Demonstration Project

CMS initiated the Florida Infusion Therapy Demonstration Project in 2007, to address a pervasive problem with clinics and solo practitioners submitting fraudulent intravenous infusion therapy claims in Florida. CMS developed automated fraud edits for those services at medically unnecessary frequencies and at lethal dosages to prevent payment for improper or fraudulent claims. During the time period of June 1, 2005, through July, 31, 2011, these edits resulted in denials totaling approximately $288.9 million.

South Florida Fraud Hot Line

CMS also continued a successful initiative aimed at increasing fraud reporting in South Florida. As part of a two-year infusion therapy demonstration, CMS established a special fraud hotline in 2007 to protect Medicare beneficiaries in South Florida from fraudulent providers of infusion therapy. As a result of the hotline's success, in FY 2009 CMS expanded the scope of this infusion therapy fraud hotline to handle all Medicare fraud-related calls in South Florida; this hotline remained in effect in FY 2011. The fraud hotline number is included on monthly Medicare Summary Notices (MSNs) sent to beneficiaries in Miami-Dade, Broward and Palm Beach counties.

Trained, bilingual, or trilingual staff fielded and routed calls, as well as acknowledged receipt of complaints in writing. A rapid response team at the ZPIC investigated the highest priority leads received from the fraud hotline within 48 hours of receipt of the call and then collaborated with CMS and/or law enforcement to pursue appropriate follow up action(s). CMS worked with its partners to conduct beneficiary outreach and education to ensure beneficiaries understood the types of fraud that may occur and how to read their MSNs to better detect potential fraudulent billings.

As of September 2011, the hotline has received more than 54,513 calls leading to 835 new fraud investigations. In addition, the ZPIC has placed 137 providers on prepayment review saving $10.7 million, revoked/deactivated 103 provider numbers, requested $58.6 million overpayments, referred 30 cases to law enforcement, and sent 106 Immediate Advisements to the HHS/OIG. Additionally, law enforcement has seized $3 million in provider bank accounts.

Durable Medical Equipment Prosthetics, Orthotics, and Supplies Stop Gap Plan

The DME Stop Gap Plan was developed in response to the continued escalation in DMEPOS fraud and the delay in implementation of DMEPOS competitive bidding. This two-year project was initiated in FY 2009 to enhance detection and prevention activities in connection with fraud, waste and abuse in Durable medical Equipment, Prosthetics, Orthotics, and Supplies

(DMEPOS) in seven high risk states (California, Florida, Illinois, Michigan, North Carolina, New York and Texas). The project is intended to address fraud involving high risk suppliers, ordering physicians, DMEPOS items, and beneficiaries in each area.

Under this project, CMS and its contractors identify and interview or conduct site visits to the highest paid/highest risk DMEPOS suppliers, ordering physicians; and utilizing beneficiaries; and identify and scrutinize the highest billed/highest risk DMEPOS equipment and supplies. Based on the findings, administrative actions, as appropriate, are initiated. The second year of the project concluded on September 30, 2011 and the results to date include onsite interviews/reviews of 5,230 high risk providers, suppliers, and beneficiaries; implementation of 15,409 claims processing edits to prevent improper payment (with associated $34.9 million in denied claims); $66.2 million in requested overpayments; 1,200 new investigations opened; and 469 suppliers revoked or deactivated.

Labs & PINs Workgroup

CMS continued to host monthly conference calls for a workgroup comprised of CMS staff nationwide, PSCs, ZPICs, the CNC, and law enforcement, including, the FBI, HHS/OIG and Railroad Retirement Board/OIG, to share information on "false front" (sham) providers and current fraudulent schemes. Monthly meetings provided invaluable intelligence on geographic shifts and cross-regional schemes. On October 13, 2010, OIG and the FBI conducted a National takedown of 73 individuals connected to related identity theft schemes. This workgroup provided significant information that contributed to the arrests. As of August 2011, workgroup activities resulted in approximately $165.8 million in Part B savings through denied claims, overpayments, administrative actions, and seizures by law enforcement.

Medical Director Support

In FY 2011, CMS was awarded HHS Wedge funding to hire additional Contractor Medical Directors (CMDs) to support CMS anti-fraud and error rate reduction efforts. Currently there are a limited number of Medical Directors who have several responsibilities including serving as expert witnesses at fraud hearings.

This project supports agency administrative actions and the HEAT initiatives by ensuring there are adequate CMDs that can serve as expert witnesses in court. The funding received in FY 2011 will be used to hire the CMDs in early FY 2012. Findings from this project will be reported in the FY 2012 HCFAC report.

Administration on Aging

In FY 2011, the Administration on Aging (AoA) was allocated $3.3 million in HCFAC funding by HHS to support infrastructure, technical assistance, and the other Senior Medicare Patrol (SMP) program support and capacity-building activities designed to enhance the effectiveness of state-wide SMP programs. SMP is funded from a separate Congressional appropriation. These dollars support SMP programs that recruit retired professionals to educate and assist Medicare beneficiaries to detect and report health care fraud, error, and abuse in the Medicare and Medicaid programs. According to the most recent annual performance report from HHS/OIG's Deputy Inspector General for Evaluation and Inspections, dated May 6, 2011, 4,964 active volunteers served the 55 SMP projects during 2010. This represents a 12 percent increase in the number of volunteers from that of 2009. These volunteers performed an essential function of this program, contributing 129,662 hours in efforts to educate beneficiaries about how to prevent and detect Medicare and Medicaid fraud within local communities.

Outreach to senior consumers is a key element of the SMP program. During 2010, SMP projects held 6,231 community outreach education events reaching close to an estimated 1.5 million people, and were responsible for close to 52,000 media airings to increase beneficiary awareness about issues related to Medicare and Medicaid integrity. During this period, 70,789 one-on-one counseling sessions were held with or on behalf of a beneficiary on a variety of issues related to potential Medicare or Medicaid fraud, error, or abuse, a 109 percent increase over that in 2009. In addition, over 298,097 beneficiaries were educated through 8,300 group educational sessions conducted by SMP programs in local communities.

Additionally, the National Hispanic SMP (NHSMP) project continued expanded efforts to prevent Medicare fraud among Hispanic older adults, a population especially vulnerable to Medicare fraud. In FY 2011, the NHSMP efforts were centered on a volunteer outreach program and community outreach and communications campaign designed for and implemented in South Florida. The NHSMP has partnered with Univision to develop and air television PSAs designed to inform the Hispanic population in South Florida that Medicare fraud is a crime. Additional print materials were developed to accompany this media campaign. In addition, the NHSMP is developing a training manual for SMP Hispanic partner organizations and volunteers, designed to be culturally and linguistically sensitive. The training materials will be disseminated to SMP projects for their use in local Hispanic communities nationwide.

As a result of educating beneficiaries, SMP projects nationwide resolved 89,612 inquiries for information or assistance in 2010 from or on behalf of beneficiaries, a 50 percent increase from 2009. This included receipt of 2,273 complex issues—i.e., beneficiary complaints requiring further research, assistance, case development, and/or referral. While the SMP program staff was able to resolve 1,661 complex issues for beneficiaries during 2010, an additional 922 of these issues, with an estimated dollar value of close to $1.5 million, were referred to law enforcement, CMS integrity contractors, state Medicaid Fraud Control Units, or other entities for further action. During this period, HHS/OIG documented that $248,064 in health care expenditures were avoided and over $39,031 in Medicare, Medicaid and other savings resulted from actions taken by the SMP program.

Since the program's inception, the program has educated over 4.2 million beneficiaries in group or one-on-one counseling sessions and has reached over 25.3 million people through community education outreach events. While SMPs make numerous referrals of potential fraud to CMS program integrity contractors, there is no mechanism for tracking the actions (investigation, prosecution, collection) required to realize actual savings to the government as a result of these referrals. Therefore, it is not possible to directly track the outcome of most of the cases reported and dollars recovered as a result of SMP program activities. Moreover, the impact of the SMP program's primary activities—education of beneficiaries to prevent health care fraud—is difficult to measure and impossible to quantify in dollars and cents. As HHS/OIG indicated in the May 2011 report:

> "We continue to emphasize that the number of beneficiaries who have learned from the Senior Medicare Patrol Projects to detect fraud, waste, and abuse and who subsequently call the OIG fraud hotline or other contacts cannot be tracked. Therefore, the projects may not be receiving full credit for savings attributable to their work. In addition, the projects are unable to track substantial savings derived from a sentinel effect, whereby fraud and errors are reduced in light of Medicare beneficiaries scrutiny of their bills."

AoA recognizes the importance of measuring the value of the SMP program impact to the fullest degree possible. Toward that end, in 2011 AoA contracted for assistance in the design of a first-ever SMP program evaluation that will assess the adequacy of current SMP performance measures, and seek to determine the most appropriate measures of SMP program value (benefits, results and impact). It is expected that the SMP evaluation will be conducted starting in 2012.

In addition, during FY 2011, AoA and HHS/OIG initiated a collaborative effort to help ensure SMP referrals of beneficiary complaints of potential fraud are received by law enforcement in a timely fashion. This has included development of processes for SMP referral of beneficiary complaints to the HHS/OIG hotline, including mechanisms for capturing outcomes related to these referrals.

Despite the factors that have limited AoA's ability to quantify the value of the SMP program in preventing, identifying, and reporting health care fraud, the OIG has documented close to $106 million in savings attributable to the program as a result of beneficiary complaints since its inception in 1997.

Office of the General Counsel

In FY 2011, the Office of the General Counsel (OGC) was allocated approximately $8.9 million in HCFAC funding by HHS to supplement OGC's efforts to support program integrity activities. OGC's efforts in FY 2011 focused heavily on program integrity review, in which OGC reviews CMS' programs and activities in order to strengthen them against potential fraud, waste, and abuse. OGC also continued to expand its litigation role in order to assist in the recovery of program funds. During FY 2011, OGC was involved in a wide range of HCFAC efforts that resulted in Government recoveries of over $1.1 billion in judgments, settlements, or other types of recoveries, savings, or receivables described elsewhere in this report.

The Affordable Care Act

The ACA significantly amends existing anti-fraud statutes. These provisions establish fundamental expectations for compliance, disclosure, transparency, and quality of care, and are matched by corresponding enforcement provisions. Some specific provisions of the ACA that particularly support HCFAC priorities and goals amend the AKS provider/supplier Medicare and Medicaid enrollment requirements, overpayment provisions to specifically invoke the FCA, and create a statutory disclosure protocol for violations of the physician self-referral prohibitions known as the "Stark Law." During FY 2011, OGC spent significant time and resources working with CMS to implement the program integrity provisions of the ACA. As new programs from the ACA were implemented, OGC was involved in working with the relevant agencies to ensure that program integrity issues were reviewed and resolved and assisted the agencies in addressing program integrity and compliance problems as they occurred.

HEAT

During FY 2011, OGC was involved in HEAT initiatives and worked closely with other HEAT members to combat fraud, waste, and abuse in the Medicare and Medicaid programs by providing advice on the myriad legal issues presented as the government works to initiate innovative antifraud programs in various hotspots throughout the country. OGC's involvement in HEAT included advising CMS on provider and supplier revocations, payment suspensions, and recoupments that arise from the initiative (as they arose, in addition to criminal and civil fraud prosecutions) and defending the administrative appeals that resulted. OGC continued to assist DOJ in prosecuting those seeking to defraud Medicare and Medicaid and defend any Federal court challenges that are brought as a result of this initiative.

FCA and *Qui Tam* Actions

OGC assisted DOJ in assessing *qui tam* actions filed under the FCA by interpreting complex Medicare and Medicaid rules and policies in order to help DOJ focus on those matters which were most likely to result in a recovery of money for the government. When DOJ filed or intervened in a FCA matter, OGC provided litigation support, including interviewing and preparing witnesses and responding to requests for documents and information. In FY 2011, OGC participated in FCA and related matters that recovered over $735 million for the government. The types of FCA cases in which OGC participated included: drug pricing manipulation; illegal marketing activity by pharmaceutical manufacturers that resulted in Medicare and Medicaid paying for drugs for indications that were not covered; underpayment of rebates to state Medicaid programs; physician self-referral and AKS violations; and provider upcoding and outlier cases.

Provider/Supplier Suspensions and Enrollment Revocations or Denials

Suspensions play a critical role in protecting against the abuse of program funds because they provide a source from which CMS can obtain recoupment after a final overpayment has been determined. Suspensions can also prevent improper payment from being made, thus avoiding the need to "chase" down these funds later. OGC advised CMS on whether to suspend payments to Medicare providers and suppliers and defended the suspensions when challenged. During FY 2011, OGC attorneys were involved in a myriad of suspension and recoupment actions, many of which involved fraudulent billings and different segments of the health care industry, including DME suppliers, ambulance companies, physicians, infusion clinics, therapists, home health agencies, and diagnostic testing facilities. FY 2011 recoveries in this area totaled over $17.4 million. OGC also represented CMS when a provider or supplier appealed CMS' denial of enrollment or revocation. During FY 2011, OGC represented CMS in numerous appeals before the Departmental Appeals Board (DAB) and typically resolved these cases without formal hearings. OGC also continued to advise CMS on the interpretation of enrollment regulations and reviewed proposed enrollment rules and manual changes.

During FY 2011, OGC also worked with CMS to finalize and then implement new regulations governing payment suspension. Previously, CMS' regulations authorized a payment suspension when CMS or its contractor possessed "reliable information that an overpayment ... exists or that the payments to be made may not be correct." The new regulations, which were promulgated pursuant to section 6402(h) of the Affordable Care Act, add to this authority and allow CMS to suspend payment to a provider or supplier pending investigation of "credible allegations of fraud." The new regulations state that "[a]n investigation of credible allegations of fraud will be considered resolved when legal action is terminated by settlement, judgment, or dismissal, or when the case is closed or dropped because of insufficient evidence to support the allegations of fraud." This rulemaking strengthens CMS' ability to protect the Trust Funds and helps the agency move away from a "pay and chase" approach to a prevention-focused approach.

Medicare Prescription Drug Program (Part D) & Medicare Advantage Program (Part C) Compliance

OGC continued to provide extensive advice to CMS on a variety of Part D and MA-related contract compliance issues, including identifying enforcement options against sponsors that are noncompliant or violate program rules, such as Marketing Guidelines. OGC reviewed compliance-related correspondence that CMS issued to Part D sponsors and MA plans in the form of warning letters, corrective action plan letters, intermediate sanction, and CMP notices and non-renewal or termination notices.

Civil Monetary Penalties

CMS has the responsibility for administering numerous CMP provisions enacted by Congress to combat fraud, waste, and abuse by enforcing program compliance and payment integrity. During FY 2011, OGC provided legal advice to CMS regarding the development and imposition of CMPs and defended CMS in numerous administrative appeals and judicial litigation resulting from these cases, recovering or establishing the right to recover over $22.5 million in CMPs.

Petitions for Remission

OGC collaborated with Federal law enforcement, including the FBI, the USAOs, the Secret Service, U.S. Postal Service, and the U.S. Marshal's Service in filing petitions for remission directed to recover assets subject either to administrative forfeiture by Federal law enforcement or civil judicial forfeiture by DOJ. Each petition set forth the background of the fraudulent scheme, the history of Medicare's payments, and how the fraudulently induced payments could be traced to the seized assets. During FY 2011, OGC petitioned these agencies to recover funds in both criminal and civil litigation matters in which Medicare was a victim of fraud involving about $20.7 million seized by law enforcement agencies.

Regulatory Review and Programmatic Advice

During FY 2011, OGC advised CMS regarding compliance related provisions of a proposed rule for the Medicare Parts C and D programs. OGG also advised CMS regarding a variety of contract compliance, immediate sanction, and civil money penalty issues, and assisted CMS with a variety of law enforcement inquiries related to Parts C and D. OGC also worked with CMS and the DOJ to defend the agency in an ongoing Federal court challenge to the 2010 immediate termination of a Medicare Part D sponsor. Further, OGC advised CMS regarding the development and implementation of the appeals process for the Part C risk adjustment data validation audit initiative. In addition, OGC provided legal counsel to CMS regarding a final rule that provides CMS with greater discretion in determining when providers and suppliers have met all federal requirements and conditions of participation in the Medicare program.

Medicaid Integrity

Continuing recent trends, OGC saw continued increasing involvement in FY 2011 in Medicaid integrity issues as CMS devoted more resources to financial reviews and oversight and as states continued to present innovative proposals to reconfigure their programs and to draw down federal financial participation at or beyond the margins of the regular Medicaid program. During FY 2011, two notable court decisions impacted our work on Medicaid integrity and state FCA recovery issues. An Alabama district court decision vacated on APA grounds CMS' State Health Official Letter outlining CMS' expectations about states' return of the Federal share when states recover in FCA actions, while a Fourth Circuit decision affirmed CMS' recovery of the Federal share stemming from Medicaid-related litigation undertaken by West Virginia. During FY 2011, OGC was successful in securing over $304 million in Medicaid program savings.

Physician Self-Referral

OGC provided valuable assistance to CMS in navigating the complexities of the Stark physician self-referral law. In FY 2011, OGC reviewed several draft Stark advisory opinions as well as various payment or coverage rules and suggested modifications necessary to avoid implicating, or to conform the regulation to, the Stark law. In addition, OGC has been instrumental in advising CMS on the newly established (by the ACA) voluntary Self Referral Disclosure Protocol, under which providers of services and supplies may self-disclose actual or potential violations of the physician self-referral statute. OGC has advised CMS on how to implement this new provision, how to apply the protocol, and how to resolve the specific disclosures (now over 100) that CMS has received.

Medicare Secondary Payer (MSP) Workload

OGC's efforts to recover conditional payments by Medicare that are the primary responsibility of other payers directly supports the HCFAC statutory goal of facilitating the enforcement of all applicable legal remedies for program fraud and abuse. During FY 2011, OGC has been successful in establishing the right to recover over $4.6 million for Medicare under the MSP program. Recent statutory changes to the MSP law have strengthened and expanded OGC's efforts in this area – to the benefit of the Medicare Trust Funds – including substantial CMPs for failure to report.

Bankruptcy Litigation

OGC protected Medicare funds when providers sought bankruptcy protections by asserting CMS' recoupment and set-off rights to collect overpayments, arguing to continue suspension or termination actions against debtors, seeking adequate assurances from the bankruptcy court that CMS' interests in the debtor's estate will be protected, arguing for the assumption of the Medicare provider agreement as an executory contract, and petitioning for administrative costs where appropriate. In FY 2011, OGC vigorously asserted CMS' interests in numerous bankruptcy and receivership actions involving physicans, hospitals, independent diagnostic test facilities, DME suppliers, nursing homes, and nursing home chains, negotiated agreements to recover overpayments, and aggressively advanced the use of Medicare's recoupment and set-off authority, collecting or establishing the right to collect over $58 million in recoveries involving bankrupt providers.

Denial of Claims and Payments

CMS and its contractors engaged in various activities and initiatives to detect and prevent abusive and fraudulent billing practices. These measures included provider and beneficiary education, use of claim sampling techniques, and a more rigorous scrutiny of claims with increased medical review. In FY 2011, OGC played a major role in advising CMS regarding the development and implementation of these types of program integrity measures and defended CMS in litigation brought by providers and suppliers who challenged these efforts. OGC continued to aggressively defend CMS and its contractors in cases seeking damages for the alleged wrongful denial of claims, for being placed on payment suspension, and for not being granted extended repayment plans.

Food and Drug Administration Pharmaceutical Fraud Program

In FY 2011, the FDA was allocated $3.4 million in HCFAC funding by HHS for the FDA Pharmaceutical Fraud Pilot Program (PFPP). The PFPP has enhanced the health care fraud-related activities of FDA's Office of Criminal Investigations (OCI) and the OGC Food and Drug Division. OCI, with the support of OGC, investigates criminal violations of the FDCA, the Prescription Drug Marketing Act, the Federal Anti-Tampering Act, and related Federal statutes.

The PFPP is designed to detect, prosecute, and prevent pharmaceutical, biologic, and medical device fraud. The PFPP gathers information from sources inside and outside FDA and focuses on fraudulent marketing schemes, application fraud, clinical trial fraud, and flagrant manufacturing-related violations related to biologics, drugs, and medical devices. The early detection and prosecution of fraudulent conduct furthers FDA's public health mission and helps reduce health care costs and deter future violators. As described below, the PFPP has identified multiple alleged medical product fraud schemes through various avenues including enhanced intra-agency coordination.

In FY 2011, FDA continued the PFPP and hired the approved complement of personnel. FDA continued the coordination and communication between criminal investigators, regulatory components of FDA, and the USAOs investigating PFPP-identified health care fraud-related investigations. In its first full fiscal year of HCFAC program activity, FDA, through its PFPP, secured two indictments relative to clinical trial fraud. In addition, 16 criminal investigations were initiated including the following:

- Four investigations involving allegations of off-label drug promotion by different manufacturers of brand name drugs;
- One investigation involving allegations of off-label drug promotion and other violative promotional issues by a manufacturer of brand name drugs including unsubstantiated superiority claims and omission of risk information;
- One investigation involving a medical device manufacturer pertaining to issues involving a recalled device product;
- One investigation involving allegations that a company withheld nonclinical studies from FDA regarding Investigational Device Exemption applications because the studies demonstrated that the products in the applications could be hazardous to patients; and
- Nine investigations involving allegations of clinical trial fraud and/or application fraud.

In regards to judicial action on clinical trial fraud, a physician and clinical research coordinator were indicted on charges of falsifying study data in a clinical trial. The pair was charged with one count of conspiracy, three counts of mail fraud, and one count of falsifying information required by the FDA. The indictment alleges the defendants were employed by a research institute that was hired by a pharmaceutical manufacturer to perform a clinical trial on a tablet for the treatment of allergies. The plans for the study called for all test subjects to be 50 years of age or older and to suffer from ragweed-induced allergy symptoms. The pharmaceutical manufacturer required that employees of the clinical trial facility who were directly involved with the study be excluded as test subjects. The defendants reported that eight test subjects were qualified, even though they knew two of the test subjects were not qualified. The two test subjects both under 50 years of age were employees at the research institute, who were using false names and dates of birth to participate in the study. The indictment alleges the defendants falsely stated physical examinations had been conducted on the two unqualified test subjects, signed false statements to FDA indicating the clinical study was being conducted in accordance with proper protocol, and arranged for the unqualified subjects to have office visits while the executive director was at lunch in order to conceal the fact that the test subjects were ineligible.

In addition, FDA developed and conducted a three day training session geared toward Special Agents, Supervisors, and Attorneys. Presenters, consisting of Special Agents, Attorneys, and FDA Center personnel, covered multiple HCFAC related topics including off-label promotion, clinical trial fraud, application fraud, and the resources and divisions within and external to FDA that would be most helpful to case agents working HCFAC cases.

Assistant Secretary for Public Affairs

In FY 2010, the Assistant Secretary for Public Affairs (ASPA) was allocated $690,894 in HCFAC funding by HHS to produce a series of live, remote events to promote the awareness of health care fraud issues before national and regional public and law enforcement audiences. Funding for this project was a direct result of feedback given at the National Fraud Summit; it addressed multiple workgroup recommendations that more be done to raise the public awareness of how health care fraud can be prevented. While funding was allocated to ASPA in FY 2010, these events occurred, and the funds were obligated, in FY 2011.

In FY 2011, ASPA produced seven events spanning several months. The events were held in Miami, Boston, Los Angeles, Detroit, Philadelphia, and New York City. The events targeted areas with a high incidence of health care fraud where DOJ and HHS are working to prevent, deter, and prosecute such fraud. These events included presentations with distinguished speakers and panel discussions, including participation by the HHS Secretary and Attorney General. Additionally, the events were webcast live and involved an open press conference for a public forum for the press to ask questions of Administration officials.

The effectiveness of outreach activities can be measured in part by the increase in website activity surrounding the dates of the conferences; for example, the government website www.stopmedicarefraud.gov experienced a 75 percent increase in activity surrounding the dates of the Boston Health Care Fraud Summit. By surveying participants, ASPA was able to measure in part the importance of government in educating the public about health care fraud. For example, in a survey of the Boston and New York Fraud Summits, over half of the respondents said they receive information about health care fraud prevention from conferences and events. Moreover, over 85 percent of survey respondents use Federal government resources, such as the website www.stopmedicarefraud.gov, to obtain information about health care fraud. The health care fraud summits have provided an open public forum to promote public awareness and stress health care cost savings potential; they have also received an overwhelmingly positive response from the media.

Additionally, an initial round of national paid advertising began in October 2010 and a second round of a national paid advertising began in August 2011 using HCFAC funding provided to ASPA in FY 2010. The advertising was targeted to Medicare beneficiaries and was designed to educate Medicare beneficiaries about the importance of keeping Medicare information private and where to go for help if fraud is suspected. The paid advertising referred beneficiaries to 1-800- MEDICARE or www.stopmedicarefraud.gov for help and ran nationally on national cable networks. This round of advertising also included targeted ethnic advertising in select markets. Local print and radio advertising ran in Russian in New York, in Spanish in Miami, and in Armenian in Los Angeles.

The Department of Justice

United States Attorneys

In FY 2011, the United States Attorney's Offices (USAOs) were allocated approximately $41.1 million in HCFAC funding to support civil and criminal health care fraud and abuse litigation, as exemplified in the Program Accomplishments section. The USAOs dedicated substantial district resources to combating health care fraud and abuse in 2011, and HCFAC allocations have supplemented those resources by providing funding for attorneys, paralegals, auditors and investigators, as well as funds for litigation of resource-intensive health care fraud cases.

The 93 United States Attorneys and their assistants, or AUSAs, are the nation's principal prosecutors of federal crimes, including health care fraud. Each district has a designated Criminal Health Care Fraud Coordinator and a Civil Health Care Fraud Coordinator. Civil and criminal health care fraud referrals are often made to USAOs through the law enforcement network described herein, and these cases are usually handled primarily by the USAOs, although the civil referrals are sometimes handled jointly with the Civil Division's Fraud Section. The other principal source of referrals of civil cases for USAOs is through the filing of *qui tam* (or whistleblower) complaints. These cases are often handled jointly with trial attorneys in the Frauds Section. USAOs also handle most criminal and civil appeals at the Federal appellate level.

USAOs play a major role in health care fraud enforcement by bringing criminal and affirmative civil cases to recover funds wrongfully taken from the Medicare Trust Funds and other taxpayer-funded health care systems as a result of fraud, waste, and abuse. Civil and criminal AUSAs litigate a wide variety of health care fraud matters, including false billings by physicians and other providers of medical services, overcharges by hospitals, Medicaid fraud, kickbacks to induce referrals of Medicare or Medicaid patients, fraud by pharmaceutical and medical device companies, home health fraud, and failure of care allegations against nursing home owners. Working closely with their partners in Civil Frauds, several civil health care fraud AUSAs have focused their efforts on pharmaceutical fraud, resulting in significant civil recoveries including: $701 million from Abbott Laboratories, Roxane Laboratories and Dey, Inc.; $600 million from GlaxoSmithKline; $60 million from Elan Corp.; and $25 million from Novo Nordisk. Most of the civil settlements were part of a global resolution, which also addressed the criminal liabilities, resulting in criminal pleas, as well as significant fines and forfeitures. The criminal portion of these investigations and resolutions was handled by criminal health care fraud AUSAs. These global settlements resolved allegations including, reporting of false and inflated drug prices, manufacturing and distributing adulterated drugs, off-label marketing and kick-backs. All of these cases are detailed earlier in this report.

Turning to other health care fraud, several of the USAOs have dedicated significant resources to investigate fraud perpetrated on our most vulnerable citizens. To this end, the USAOs have partnered with Civil Frauds in the Elder Justice and Nursing Home Initiative to address elder abuse and neglect, and many USAOs have devoted resources to investigating home health fraud. As a result of these efforts, Maxim Healthcare Services, Inc., one of the nation's leading providers of home health care services, executed a DPA, and agreed to pay more than $150 million to resolve criminal and civil charges relating to a nationwide scheme to defraud Medicaid programs and Veterans Affairs program.

The USAOs partner with the Criminal Division in the Strike Forces, which are currently operating in nine USAOs across the country. Each USAO has dedicated several AUSAs and support personnel to work with Criminal Division attorneys in this important initiative. The MFSFs use data analysis to identify high-billing levels in health care hot spots so that emerging or migrating schemes can be targeted. The significant successes of the MFSFs are detailed earlier in this report.

Special Focus Teams, consisting of criminal and civil AUSAs, paralegals, and auditors, are operational in three districts and focus on pharmaceutical, biologics, and medical device fraud. The teams have contributed significantly to the success of the pharmaceutical investigations and recoveries this year. To increase the capacity of other districts to successfully litigate these complex health care fraud cases, the Special Focus Teams have organized monthly training Webinars and serve as advisors for the USAO community in the various complex areas of health care fraud.

In addition to the positions funded by HCFAC, the Executive Office for United States Attorneys' Office of Legal Education (OLE) uses HCFAC funds to train AUSAs and other DOJ attorneys, as well as paralegals, investigators, and auditors in the investigation and prosecution of health care fraud. In 2011, OLE offered an Affirmative Civil Enforcement (ACE) Seminar, which included training on health care fraud, and was attended by over 100 AUSAs and DOJ trial attorneys. In addition, an ACE Conference, with a heavy concentration on health care fraud issues, was offered for paralegals, auditors, and investigators. Many USAO attorneys, investigators, auditors, and paralegals serve as faculty at these OLE trainings, and also participate in other Federal, state, and private health care fraud seminars.

Criminal Prosecutions

In FY 2011, the USAOs received 1,110 new criminal matters involving 2,561 defendants, and had 1,873 health care fraud criminal matters pending,[14] involving 3,118 defendants. The USAOs filed criminal charges in 489 cases involving 1,430 defendants, and obtained 743 federal health care fraud related convictions.

Civil Matters and Cases

In FY 2011, the USAOs had opened 977 new civil health care fraud investigations. At the end of FY 2011, the USAOs had 1,069 civil health care fraud investigations pending.

Civil Division

In FY 2011, the Civil Division received approximately $22.3 million in HCFAC funding to support the health care fraud activities of the Commercial Litigation Branch's Fraud Section and the Consumer Protection Branch. This amount also included funding to support the Department of Justice's Elder Justice and Nursing Home Initiative.

The Commercial Litigation Branch's Fraud Section

The Civil Division's Commercial Litigation Branch (and, specifically, its Fraud Section) investigates health care fraud allegations and brings actions under the FCA to recover money on behalf of defrauded federal health care programs including Medicare, Medicaid, TRICARE, and the FEHBP. Working closely with the USAOs, HHS/OIG, and other law enforcement agencies, the Commercial Litigation Branch's Fraud Section has recovered over $1 billion almost every year since 2000 and $2.35 billion in FY 2011 alone.

The Commercial Litigation Branch's Fraud Section investigates and resolves matters involving a wide array of health care providers and schemes. In recent years, pharmaceutical fraud cases have constituted a significant component of the Section's health care fraud efforts. These cases are commonly nationwide in scope, involve legally and factually complex questions, and routinely require the dedication of significant resources to investigate and resolve. As mentioned previously in this report, these cases included GlaxoSmithKline, which paid $600 million to resolve FCA and related state claims related to its faulty manufacturing practices and distribution of certain adulterated drugs. They also included Abbott Laboratories, Roxane Laboratories and Dey, Inc., which paid over $700 million to settle FCA claims that they had knowingly reported inflated prices for their drugs products and caused Medicare and Medicaid to overpay for those drugs as a result.

In addition to pharmaceutical fraud, the Commercial Litigation Branch's Fraud Section investigates hospitals, physicians, and other providers for providing and billing Medicare for medically unreasonable and unnecessary services. These have included the seven hospitals mentioned herein that paid over $6 million to resolve FCA claims for submitting false claims related to medically unnecessary inpatient kyphoplasty claims, as well as a physician who paid $5.7 million to resolve claims involving medically unnecessary radiation oncology services.

The Commercial Litigation Branch's Fraud Section also investigates cases arising from violations of the AKS or Stark Law, where hospitals, pharmaceutical companies, other suppliers pay kickbacks to doctors and others in order to induce service referrals of Medicare or Medicaid patients. These included the Medline Industries, Inc. case, where the company paid $85 million to resolve allegations that it paid kickbacks to induce health care providers to purchase, lease, or order medical goods and supplies from it. It also included the St. Jude Medical, Inc. matter, in which the company paid $16 million to resolve allegations that it paid kickbacks to induce physicians to implant its pacemakers and defibrillators.

In addition to its investigative responsibilities, the Commercial Litigation Branch's Fraud Section plays a critical role supporting and providing guidance to its health care fraud partners. It regularly provides training and guidance to AUSAs and agents on the FCA and health care fraud issues. The Section works closely with HHS/OIG, Office of General Counsel, in all settlements of health care fraud allegations in order to ensure that the administrative remedies possessed by HHS are appropriately considered and to enable the negotiation of compliance terms that diminish the risk that the offending conduct will be repeated. The Section also collaborates with and counsels CMS and HHS/OIG on interagency initiatives and proposed rules and regulations.

The Elder Justice and Nursing Home Initiative, which is housed in the Civil Division, coordinates and supports law enforcement efforts to combat elder abuse, neglect, and financial exploitation. The Initiative supports law enforcement efforts by maintaining an information bank of Elder Justice related materials (including briefs, opinions, indictments, plea agreements, subpoenas templates); funding medical reviewers, auditors, and other consultants to assist DOJ attorneys and AUSAs in their nursing home and/or long term care facility cases; hosting quarterly teleconferences with DOJ attorneys and AUSAs across the country to discuss issues or developments in connection with our nursing home and failure of care cases; and coordinating nationwide investigations of skilled nursing facilities. Moreover, in January 2011, the Initiative developed and organized the very first Elder Justice training program at the National Advocacy Center. This two day training focused on instructing AUSAs and agents on how to investigate, develop, and if necessary, litigate, "failure of care" cases against nursing homes and long term care providers. In addition to supporting law enforcement efforts, the Initiative continues to fund research projects awarded by the Office of Justice Programs, National Institute of Justice, to study the abuse, neglect, and exploitation of elderly individuals and residents of residential care facilities.

The Consumer Protection Branch

The Consumer Protection Branch (CPB) investigates and prosecutes drug and device manufacturers and individuals who are illegally promoting and distributing unapproved, misbranded, and adulterated drugs and devices in violation of the FDCA. CPB works closely with our counterparts in the Commercial Litigation Branch's Fraud Section, the USAOs, and the FDA on a wide variety of health care fraud matters. In recent years, CPB has convicted dozens of companies and individuals. The prosecutions resulted in significant jail terms and fines, penalties, and forfeitures totaling in the billions of dollars.

In the area of pharmaceutical and device fraud, CPB coordinates complex investigations with districts nationwide, staffing the cases directly as well as providing assistance to USAOs.

Because these investigations are complicated, both legally and factually, they demand significant resources. The recent prosecution of Marc Hermelin, a pharmaceutical company executive, is an example of the sort of complex health care fraud investigations the Consumer Protection Branch handles with USAOs. This case was handled jointly with the USAO for the Eastern District of Missouri. Mr. Hermelin, the chairman of the board and CEO of KV Pharmaceutical Company and an officer of KV's subsidiary, Ethex, pled guilty to two misdemeanor counts of introducing a misbranded pain relief and opiate drug, morphine sulfate tablets, into interstate commerce in violation of the FDCA. The morphine sulfate included oversized tablets, which contained more active ingredient of morphine than was specified in its labeling, rendering the tablets misbranded under the FDCA. In 2010, Ethex also pled guilty to two felony counts of failing to file field alerts with the FDA regarding manufacturing problems that led to the oversized tablets. The company paid a total of $27.6 million in fines, restitution, and forfeiture. By virtue of his roles at KV and Ethex, Hermelin was a "responsible corporate officer" with the authority and responsibility to prevent and correct FDCA violations at both companies. Hermelin was sentenced to 17 days in jail, was ordered to pay a $1 million fine, and was ordered to forfeit $900,000.

In addition to prosecuting legitimate businesses and individuals for health care offenses, CPB prosecutes illegitimate businesses and charlatans selling fake cures. For example, in FY 2011, CPB prosecuted four individuals and one company who were convicted of conspiracy to market medical equipment and drug treatments for a nonexistent epidemic of Lyme disease. The company functioned as an "alternative" medical provider that disseminated materials claiming that Lyme disease was "the undiagnosed plague of the 21st century" and was a contributing factor in many chronic illnesses. Using misrepresentations and misleading information, the defendants conspired to violate the FDCA by selling a microscope that supposedly would diagnose Lyme disease, as well as a treatment that included injecting patients with drugs that were neither FDA reviewed nor approved. A Kansas doctor used one of these medicines in one of his patients, resulting in that patient's death.

CPB has also been a leader in investigating and prosecuting Internet pharmacies, which is, in many ways, the leading edge of health care fraud in the United States. The Internet now provides an avenue for the illegal dissemination of prescription drugs and controlled substances for drug abusers and others who divert drugs. Website owners often hire doctors and pharmacists who are willing to authorize and dispense prescriptions based on an online questionnaire, without any legitimate doctor-patient relationship, thereby permitting these websites to operate as online "pill mills." Through the FDCA, CPB prosecutes those who unlawfully distribute prescription drugs and controlled substances over the Internet. As a result of its leadership in this area, CPB is now a primary source for legal advice to prosecutors around the country pursuing such cases.

In addition, CPB provides expertise and guidance in the prosecution of those selling counterfeit drugs—which are often sold online and are a growing problem in the United States and abroad. In addition to advising USAOs on this issue, CPB also serves on the Attorney General's Task Force on Intellectual Property, which has made it a priority to improve law enforcement with respect to counterfeit products, such as drugs and devices, which threaten the public health and safety.

Criminal Division

In FY 2011, the Criminal Division was allocated $5.8 million in HCFAC funding to support criminal health care fraud litigation and interagency coordination, which is carried out primarily by two sections with the Criminal Division: the Fraud Section and the Organized Crime and Gang Section (OCGS).

The Fraud Section

The Fraud Section initiates and coordinates complex health care fraud prosecutions and supports the USAOs with legal and investigative guidance and training, and trial attorneys to prosecute health care fraud cases. Beginning in March 2007, the Criminal Division's Fraud Section, working with the local USAOs, the FBI and law enforcement partners in HHS/OIG, and state and local law enforcement agencies, launched the Medicare Fraud Strike Force in Miami-Dade County, Florida, to prosecute individuals and entities that do not provide legitimate health care services, but exist solely for the purpose of defrauding Medicare and other Government health care programs. Since 2007, DOJ and HHS have expanded the Strike Force to nine cities. In FY 2011, the Fraud Section continued to provide attorney staffing, litigation support, as well as leadership and management oversight for numerous Strike Force prosecutions in eight of the nine cities. A summary of the Fraud Section's key litigation accomplishments in FY 2011 follows:

- Opened or filed 44 new health care fraud cases involving charges against 152 defendants who collectively billed the Medicare and Medicaid programs more than $577 million;
- Obtained 88 guilty pleas and litigated 11 jury trials, winning guilty verdicts against 19 defendants;[15]
- Prison sentences imposed in the Section's health care fraud cases during the year averaged more than 53 months; and
- Court-ordered restitution, forfeiture and fines exceeded $184 million.

Fraud Section attorneys staffed and coordinated most of the Division's health care fraud litigation through the existing Medicare Fraud Strike Force teams in Miami, Los Angeles, Detroit, Houston, Brooklyn, Baton Rouge, and Tampa, and by implementing the new Strike Force phase in Dallas during FY 2011.[16]

Section attorneys coordinated two major multi-district Strike Force arrest takedowns carried out during the fiscal year and handled several of the investigations and indictments that were filed in these operations.

On February 17, 2011, Fraud Section and USAO Strike Force prosecutors unsealed charges against 115 defendants in nine cities, including doctors, nurses, health care company owners and executives, and others for their alleged participation in Medicare fraud schemes involving more than $240 million in false billing. More than 700 law enforcement agents from the FBI, HHS/OIG, multiple Medicaid Fraud Control Units, and other state and local law enforcement agencies participated in the operation, which was the largest-ever federal health care fraud takedown. In addition to making arrests, agents also executed 16 search warrants across the country in connection with ongoing Strike Force investigations.

On September 7, 2011, the Fraud Section and USAO Strike Force prosecutors unsealed charges against 91 defendants in eight cities, including doctors, nurses, health care company owners and executives, and others for their alleged participation in Medicare fraud schemes involving more than $290 million in false billing. This was the largest-ever federal health care fraud takedown, as measured by total fraudulent billings. In addition to making arrests, agents also executed 18 search warrants across the country in connection with ongoing Strike Force investigations.

In addition to Medicare Fraud Strike Force cases, the Fraud Section handles other types of complex criminal health care fraud litigation. Often, such cases are handled in a parallel manner by Fraud Section prosecutors along with DOJ Civil Division attorneys and/or AUSAs from the USAOs.

In December 2010, Kos Pharmaceuticals, a subsidiary of Abbott Laboratories, agreed to pay more than $41 million to resolve criminal and civil liability arising from conduct relating to its drugs Advicor and Niaspan. Kos also entered into a DPA and agreed to the filing of a criminal information in the Middle District of Louisiana charging the company with one count of conspiracy to violate the AKS. According to the criminal information, Kos conspired to violate the AKS by agreeing to pay physicians kickbacks in exchange for their writing prescriptions for Kos drugs. Specifically, two doctors proposed that they would endorse the use of Kos products, including Advicor, for the treatment of cholesterol in exchange for a series of payments. From 2002 to 2004, Kos made a series of payments to the two doctors or a third party intermediary in the form of "sponsorship" of continuing medical education classes conducted by the doctors and purported speakers' fees. Kos agreed to pay a $3.4 million criminal fine as a condition of the DPA. The department agreed to enter into a DPA with Kos based in part on the company's undertaking of a thorough internal investigation of misconduct; its reporting of information from the investigation to the department on a regular basis; its continued and ongoing cooperation with the department's investigation of the matter; and in recognition of the remedial measures undertaken by the company.

The Delaware-based company also agreed to pay more than $38 million to settle civil allegations under the FCA that Kos offered and paid doctors, other medical professionals, physician groups and managed care organizations, illegal kickbacks in the form of money, free travel, grants, honoraria and other valuable goods and services, in violation of the AKS to get them to prescribe or recommend Niaspan and Advicor. In addition, the United States contends that Kos promoted the sale and use of Advicor for use as first-line therapy for management of mixed dyslipidemias (a disruption of the lipids in the blood). Such an off-label use was not approved by the FDA nor was it a medically-accepted indication for which the United States and state Medicaid programs provided coverage for Advicor. The Federal share of the civil settlement is $33.7 million and the state Medicaid share exceeds $4.4 million.

In addition to health care fraud litigation, the Fraud Section also provided legal guidance to FBI and HHS/OIG agents, health program agency staff, AUSAs, and other Criminal Division attorneys on criminal, civil, and administrative tools to combat health care fraud. From September 28 through September 30, the Fraud Section hosted a three day health care fraud training conference for approximately 175 federal prosecutors, FBI agents, HHS/OIG agents, and others. The Fraud Section also provided advice and written materials on patient medical record confidentiality and disclosure issues, and coordinated referrals of possible criminal HIPAA privacy violations from the HHS Office for Civil Rights; monitored and coordinated DOJ responses to legislative proposals, major regulatory initiatives, and enforcement policy matters; reviewed and commented on health care provider requests to the HHS/OIG for advisory opinions, and consulted with the HHS/OIG on draft advisory opinions; worked with CMS to improve Medicare contractors' fraud detection, referrals to law enforcement for investigation, and case development work; and prepared and distributed to all USAOs and FBI field offices periodic summaries of recent and significant health care fraud cases.

The Organized Crime and Gang Section (OCGS)

The Criminal Division's Organized Crime and Gang Section (OCGS) supports investigations and prosecutions of fraud and abuse targeting the 2.6 million private sector health plans sponsored by employers and/or unions, as well as investigations and prosecutions of health care frauds perpetrated by domestic and international organized crime groups.

Private sector employment based group health plans are the leading source of health care coverage for individuals not covered by Medicare or Medicaid. OCGS attorneys provide litigation support and advice to AUSAs and criminal investigative agencies to combat corruption and abuse of such private employment based group health plans covered by the Employee Retirement Income Security Act (ERISA), including health care fraud schemes by corrupt entities that sell unlicensed health insurance products and health benefit frauds in violation of the prevailing wage fringe benefit laws and regulations.

OCGS attorneys provide health care fraud and abuse training and legal guidance to AUSAs and to criminal investigators and agents of the Department of Labor's Employee Benefits Security Administration and Office of Inspector General. Such guidance and training has covered prosecutions involving abuses targeting private sector employee health plans subject to ERISA, health plans sponsored by labor organizations and multiple employer welfare arrangements, as well as the use of the Racketeering Influenced and Corrupt Organizations (RICO) statute in prosecuting Medicare or Medicaid fraud or private sector health care frauds. OCGS drafts and coordinates criminal legislative initiatives affecting employee health benefit plans and reviews and comments on legislative proposals affecting employment based health benefit plans.

OCGS attorneys provide litigation support and advice in the investigation and prosecution of health care fraud perpetrated by domestic and international organized crime groups through the long-standing Organized Crime Strike Force Units located within various USAOs. For example, an OCGS attorney is teamed with the OC Strike Force Chief in the Southern District of Florida to prosecute a health care fraud perpetrated by a Eurasian organized crime group with alleged ties to Russia and Armenia. In February 2011, this prosecution was brought as part of a three city crackdown on activities of Armenian Power, an international organized crime group. The health care fraud schemes involved chiropractic clinics that allegedly paid individuals to refer "patients" of staged accidents. The clinics then billed private automobile insurance carriers for treatments that were either not medically necessary or were not provided.

OCGS is also working to improve strategic coordination in the identification and prosecution of domestic and international organized crime groups engaged in sophisticated frauds posing a threat to the health care industry.

Civil Rights Division

In FY 2011, the Civil Rights Division was allocated approximately $5.5 million in HCFAC funding to support Civil Rights Division litigation activities related to health care fraud and abuse. The Civil Rights Division pursues relief affecting public, residential health care facilities and service systems. The Division has also established an initiative to eliminate abuse and grossly substandard care in public, Medicare and Medicaid funded nursing homes and other long-term care facilities. Consistent with the Supreme Court's decision in *Olmstead v. L.C.,* 527 U.S. 581 (1999), the Division has also undertaken initiatives to eliminate the needless institutionalization of individuals who require health care supports and services.

The Division plays a critical role in the HCFAC Program. The Special Litigation Section of the Civil Rights Division is the sole DOJ component responsible for the Civil Rights of Institutionalized Persons Act, 42 U.S.C. § 1997 (CRIPA). CRIPA authorizes the investigation of conditions of confinement at state and local residential institutions (including facilities for persons with developmental disabilities or mental illness, and nursing homes) and initiation of civil action for injunctive relief to remedy a pattern or practice of violations of the Constitution or Federal statutory rights. The review of conditions in facilities for persons who have mental illness, facilities for persons with developmental disabilities, and nursing homes comprises a significant portion of the program.

The Disability Rights Section of the Civil Rights Division has primary enforcement authority for the Americans with Disabilities Act (ADA). Title II of the ADA authorizes investigation of allegations of discrimination by public entities against individuals with disabilities, including discrimination in the form of needless institutionalization of persons who require health care supports and services. *See Olmstead v. L.C.,* 527 U.S. 581 (1999). Title II also authorizes the initiation of civil action to remedy discrimination in violation of the ADA. Both the Special Litigation Section and the Disability Rights Section have undertaken initiatives to combat the unjustified institutionalization of persons with disabilities.

The Special Litigation and Disability Rights Sections work collaboratively with the USAOs and HHS.

Fiscal Year 2011 Accomplishments

Special Litigation Section staff conducted preliminary reviews of conditions and services at 16 health care facilities in 13 states during FY 2011. The task in preliminary inquiries is to determine whether there is sufficient information supporting allegations of unlawful conditions and needless institutionalization to warrant formal investigation under CRIPA. The Section reviews information pertaining to areas such as abuse and neglect, medical and mental health care, use of restraints, fire and environmental safety, and placement in the most integrated setting appropriate to individual needs. Separately, in FY 2011, the Section opened or continued formal investigations, entered remedial agreements, or monitored existing remedial agreements regarding 79 health care facilities in 25 states, the District of Columbia, the Territory of Guam, and the Commonwealth of Puerto Rico.

The Section found that conditions and practices at three state facilities for persons with mental illness, one county nursing facility, and one state facility for persons with intellectual and developmental disabilities violate the residents' Federal constitutional and statutory rights. Those facilities are: Delaware Psychiatric Center, in New Castle, DE; New Hampshire Hospital and Glencliff Home, in Concord and Benton, NH, respectively; Maple Lawn Nursing Home, in Palmyra, MO; and, Central Virginia Training Center, in Lynchburg, VA.

In Fiscal Year 2011, the Section commenced investigations of 12 Mississippi facilities for persons with intellectual and developmental disabilities and/or mental illness, including: Boswell Regional Center, in Magee, MS; Ellisville State School, in Ellisville, MS; Hudspeth Regional Center, in Pearl, MS; Southern Mississippi Regional Center, in Long Beach, MS; Mississippi Adolescent Center, in Brookhaven, MS; North Mississippi Regional Center, in Oxford, MS; Mississippi State Hospital, in Whitfield, MS; South Mississippi State Hospital, in Purvis, MS; Central Mississippi Residential Center, in Newton, MS; East Mississippi State Hospital, in Meridian, MS; North Mississippi State Hospital, in Tupelo, MS; and the Specialized Treatment Center, in Gulfport, MS.

The Section entered two settlement agreements to resolve its investigations of eight state operated facilities for persons with mental illness. Those facilities are: Georgia Regional Hospital, in Atlanta; Georgia Regional Hospital, in Savannah; Northwest Georgia Regional Hospital, in Rome; East Central Regional Hospital, in Augusta; Central State Hospital, in Milledgeville; Southwestern State Hospital, in Thomasville; West Central Georgia Regional Hospital, in Columbus, GA; and Delaware Psychiatric Center, in New Castle, DE. In addition, the Section resolved its investigation of William F. Green Veterans Nursing Home, in Bay Minette, AL, through a private agreement.

The Section continued its investigations of 13 residential facilities for persons with intellectual and developmental disabilities, including: Sonoma Developmental Center, in Eldridge, CA; Lanterman Developmental Center, in Pomona, CA; Rainier Residential Rehabilitation Center, in Buckley, WA; Bellefontaine Developmental Center, in St. Louis, MO; Northwest Habilitation Center, in St. Louis, MO; Rosewood Center, in Owings Mills, MD; Clyde L. Choate Developmental Center, in Anna, IL; Howe Developmental Center, in

Tinley Park, IL; Central Virginia Training Center, in Lynchburg, VA, and, five Arkansas facilities, including:

Arkadelphia Human Development Center, in Arkadelphia, AR; Alexander Human Development Center, in Alexander, AR; Booneville Human Development Center, in Booneville, AR; Jonesboro Human Development Center, in Jonesboro, AR; and Southeast Arkansas Human Development Center, in Warren, AR.

The Section also continued its investigations of seven facilities for persons with mental illness, including Oregon State Hospital, in Salem, OR; Delaware State Psychiatric Center, in New Castle, DE; Ancora Psychiatric Hospital, in Winslow, NJ; and, four facilities in North Carolina, including John Umstead Hospital in Butner; Dorothea Dix Hospital in Raleigh; Cherry Hospital in Goldsboro; and Broughton Hospital in Morgantown.

The Section also continued its investigations of William F. Green State Veterans' Nursing Home, in Bay Minette, AL; Maple Lawn Nursing Home, in Palmyra, MO; LaSalle Nursing Home, in Ottowa, IL; and, Casa del Veteranos, in Juana Diaz, PR. In some of these matters, the Section is reviewing voluntary compliance to improve conditions.

The Section monitored the implementation of remedial agreements for 20 facilities for persons with intellectual and developmental disabilities: Clover Bottom Developmental Center, in Nashville, TN; Greene Valley Developmental Center, in Greeneville, TN; Harold Jordan Center, in Nashville, TN; Arlington Developmental Center, in Arlington, TN; Woodbridge Developmental Center, in Woodbridge, NJ; Oakwood Community Center, in Somerset, KY; Beatrice State Developmental Center, in Beatrice, NE; Lubbock State Supported Living Center, in Lubbock, TX; Denton State Supported Living Center, in Denton, TX; Abilene State Supported Living Center, in Abilene, TX; Austin State Supported Living Center, in Austin, TX; Brenham State Supported Living Center, in Brenham, TX; Corpus Christi State Supported Living Center, in Corpus Christi, TX; El Paso State Supported Living Center, in El Paso, TX; Lufkin State Supported Living Center, in Lufkin, TX; Mexia State Supported Living Center, in Mexia, TX; Richmond State Supported Living Center, in Richmond, TX; Rio Grande State Supported Living Center, in Harlingen, TX; San Angelo State Supported Living Center, in Carlsbad, TX; San Antonio State Supported Living Center, in San Antonio, TX. These remedial agreements include the provision of adequate community supports and services.

The Section also monitored the implementation of remedial agreements regarding 16 state-operated residential facilities for persons with mental illness: Kings County Hospital Center, in Brooklyn, NY; Guam Mental Health Unit, in the Territory of Guam; Vermont State Hospital, in Waterbury, VT; Metropolitan State Hospital, in Norwalk, CA; Napa State Hospital, in Napa, CA; Atascadero State Hospital, in Atascadero, CA; Patton State Hospital, in Patton, CA; St. Elizabeth's Hospital, Washington, D.C.; Georgia Regional Hospital, in Atlanta, GA; Georgia Regional Hospital, in Savannah, GA; Northwest Georgia Regional Hospital, in Rome, GA; Central State Hospital, in Milledgeville, GA; Southwest State Hospital, in Thomasville, GA; West Central Georgia Hospital, in Columbus, GA; East Central Georgia Regional Hospital, in Augusta, GA; and, Connecticut Valley Hospital, in Middletown, CT. These remedial agreements include the provision of adequate community supports and services.

In addition, the Section continued its monitoring of four nursing facilities, including Reginald P. White Skilled Nursing Facility, in Meridian, MS; C.M. Tucker Nursing Care Center, in Columbia, SC; Ft. Bayard Medical Center, in Ft. Bayard, NM; and, Laguna Honda Hospital and Rehabilitation Center, in San Francisco, CA.

The Disability Rights Section commenced two statewide investigations. It is investigating whether the State of Utah is institutionalizing persons with physical disabilities and brain injuries in nursing homes unnecessarily, or placing individuals in the community at risk of unnecessary and costly institutionalization, in violation of the ADA. It also opened an investigation of North Carolina's mental health service system, in response to allegations that the state's service system relies needlessly on costly, segregated institutions called adult care homes as settings in which to provide services to people with mental illness who could instead be served more appropriately in community settings. Following an eight month investigation, the Section issued a findings letter to the State of North Carolina notifying it of the Section's findings that it violates the ADA by planning, structuring and administering its mental health service system to deliver services to thousands of persons with mental illness in institutional settings rather than in more appropriate, integrated settings.

The Section moved to intervene in two *Olmstead* actions. The Section moved to intervene in *Jones v. Arnold,* (M.D. Fla.), a proposed class action involving claims under the ADA that the State of Florida failed to provide community-based services to persons with spinal injuries, placing them at risk of unnecessary and more costly institutionalization. The case was voluntarily dismissed without prejudice. The Section also moved to intervene in *Steward, et al. v. Perry, et al.,* (W.D. Tex.) regarding the State of Texas' alleged practice of unnecessarily institutionalizing individuals with developmental disabilities in nursing facilities, and placing others at risk of needless institutionalization, in violation of the ADA.

As plaintiff-intervenor in Disability Advocates, Inc. v. Paterson (E.D.N.Y.), the Section participated in the implementation of a court-ordered remedy requiring the State of New York to provide community-based services to thousands of persons with mental illness who are unnecessarily institutionalized in segregated, costly facilities called adult homes. The remedy was subsequently stayed pending appeal.

The Section is conducting preliminary reviews of services and programs in three states to determine whether there is sufficient information supporting allegations of noncompliance with the ADA's integration mandate to warrant a formal investigation.

The Division filed fourteen statements of interest or *amicus* briefs in litigation raising issues of needless institutionalization in Alabama, California, Florida, Georgia, Louisiana, Mississippi, Missouri, New Jersey, Pennsylvania, Tennessee, Texas and Washington. These briefs have addressed a wide range of issues, including unnecessary institutionalization of individuals in state-run and private institutions and cuts to community services placing individuals at risk of unnecessary, and more costly, institutionalization.

The Division released a technical assistance document providing answers to frequently asked questions regarding the Department's positions on the ADA's integration mandate and the Olmstead decision. The document is designed to assist individuals in understanding their rights under title II of the ADA and to assist state and local governments in complying with the ADA. The Division also launched a new website, www.ada.gov/Olmstead, providing information about the integration mandate, the Supreme Court's Olmstead decision and the Division's Olmstead enforcement efforts.

APPENDIX

Federal Bureau of Investigation Mandatory Funding & Discretionary Funding

In FY 2011, the FBI was allocated $132.3 million in funding, including $128.4 million from HIPAA and $3.9 million from discretionary HCFAC, for health care fraud enforcement. This yearly appropriation is used to support 794 positions (477 Agent, 317 Support). In FY 2011, the FBI initiated 923 new health care fraud investigations and had 2,690 pending investigations. FBI-led investigations resulted in 736 criminal health care fraud convictions and 1,676 indictments and informations being filed in FY 2011. In FY 2011, FBI health care fraud (HCF) investigations resulted in the operational disruption of 238 criminal fraud organizations, and the dismantlement of the criminal hierarchy of more than 67 HCF criminal enterprises.

The FBI is the primary investigative agency involved in the fight against health care fraud that has jurisdiction over both the federal and private insurance programs. Each of the 56 FBI field offices has personnel assigned specifically to investigate health care fraud matters. With national health care expenditures projected to exceed $2.7 trillion dollars in FY 2011, it is especially important to coordinate all investigative efforts to combat the significant fraud and abuse within the health care system. The FBI leverages its resources in both the private and public arenas through investigative partnerships with agencies such as HHS/OIG, the FDA, the DEA, the Defense Criminal Investigative Service, the Office of Personnel Management, the Internal Revenue Service, state Medicaid Fraud Control Units, and other state and local agencies. On the private side, the FBI is actively involved with national groups, such as the National Health Care Anti-Fraud Association, the National Insurance Crime Bureau, as well as many other professional associations and private insurance investigative units.

Health care fraud investigations are considered a high priority within the FBI White Collar Crime Program and the efforts of field offices are reviewed for effectiveness and compliance. In addition to being a partner in the majority of investigations listed in the body of this report, FBI field offices throughout the U.S. have pro-actively addressed significant health care fraud threats through coordinated initiatives, task forces, working groups, and undercover operations. These activities identify and pursue investigations against the most egregious offenders, which included criminal enterprises and other crime groups.

In an effort to ensure sufficient FBI HCF resources are dedicated to address priority threats within the health care system for which the FBI has primary responsibility, the FBI established national priorities. During FY 2011, the FBI's top HCF Program National Priorities were Government Sponsored and Private Insurance Programs. Accordingly, over approximately 85 percent of FBI cases primarily involve government sponsored and private insurance program fraud. The FBI also investigated violations involving drug diversion, Internet pharmacy, and other investigations that did not include billings to government sponsored or private insurance programs.

A review of the threats to the health care system reveals that many schemes target multiple FBI HCF Program National Priority areas, and individual schemes may have considerable impact on the health care system. In response to these threats the FBI has enhanced its focus on threats to government sponsored and private insurance programs associated with large scale conspiracies and major providers, in addition to combating traditional provider fraud.

Large scale conspiracies include criminal enterprises and other crime groups involving significant losses, or potential losses, to health care benefit programs. The criminal activity of these groups can cross multiple federal districts and have included the sharing/selling of beneficiary information, the sharing/selling of referring provider identifiers, and kickback schemes involving invoices, referrals, and medical services/products. It is not unusual for more complex large scale conspiracies to conduct other criminal activity in addition to health care fraud. The potential extent of this type of criminal activity was noted in the October 2010 unsealing of indictments of seventy-three defendants, including a number of alleged members and associates of an Armenian-American organized crime enterprise, in five judicial districts with various health care fraud-related crimes involving more than $163 million in fraudulent billings. The FBI is committed to addressing this crime problem through the disruption, dismantlement and prosecution of those involved in criminal enterprises and other organized criminal activities.

Major Providers can include companies, corporations, hospitals, provider groups, and other groups able to significantly bill, or effect billing, to health care benefit programs. The related schemes are frequently complex and challenging to identify. A principal source of referrals on these schemes is the filing of *qui tams*. In FY 2011, the FBI continued to aggressively expand its involvement in *qui tam* investigations. Significant qui tam investigations for FY 2011 included the following global resolution: $750 million for SB Pharmco Puerto Rico Inc. (a subsidiary of GlaxoSmithKline, PLC) and the over $313 million for Forest Pharmaceuticals Inc. In addition to the work completed at the field office level and in response to this substantial and increasing threat, the FBI will establish a centralized squad to provide investigative assistance on these types of cases nationwide. The FBI will coordinate this effort with the DOJ, HHS/OIG, and the FDA.

In FY 2011, the FBI continued to staff and support Medicare Strike Force operations worked in conjunction with DOJ Criminal Division's Fraud Section, local USAOs, HHS/OIG, and state and local law enforcement agencies. The FBI has assigned a significant number of agents to Strike Forces in Miami, New York City, Houston, Tampa, Detroit, Los Angeles, Baton Rouge, Dallas, and Chicago. These Strike Forces have effectively investigated and prosecuted individuals and entities that do not provide legitimate health care services, but exist solely for the purpose of defrauding Medicare and other Government health care programs. The continued support of Medicare Strike Force operations is a top priority for the FBI.

In addition to its investigative efforts, the FBI actively provides training and guidance on health care matters. The FBI has teamed with the DOJ, the United States Attorneys, and HHS to provide training in the priority threat areas of health care fraud. FBI sponsored training included innovative methods of employing sophisticated and advanced investigative techniques; basic HCF training for FBI special agent and professional staff newly assigned to HCF; sessions on new and current HCF trends and issues; and training for FBI Forensic Accountants. FBI personnel were also provided the opportunity to attend training offered by other government agencies and the private sector. In FY 2011, more than 400 FBI health care fraud investigators and analysts received training. FBI personnel also conducted a wide range of training for external audiences, including personnel involved in the investigation of health care fraud matters and industry representatives.

Funding received by the FBI is used to pay direct and indirect personnel-related costs associated with the 794 funded positions. Funds not used directly for personnel matters, are used to provide operational support for major health care fraud investigations, national initiatives, training, specialized equipment, expert witness testimony, and Strike Force operations.

Return-on-Investment Calculation

- The Return-on-Investment (ROI) for the HCFAC program is calculated by dividing the total monetary results to the Federal government (not including relator payments) by the annual appropriation for the HCFAC Account in a given year.
- The monetary results include deposits and transfers to the Medicare Part A Trust Fund and the Treasury, as well as restitution and compensatory damages to Federal agencies.
- The HCFAC Account is made up of three funding sources: mandatory funding for HHS and DOJ, including HHS/OIG, appropriated through Section 1817(k)(3)(A) of the Social Security Act; mandatory funding for FBI activities appropriated through Section 1817(k)(3)(B) of the

Social Security Act; and discretionary funding for the HCFAC Account appropriated through the annual Labor-HHS-Education appropriation. FBI mandatory HIPAA funding is included in ROI calculations given the important role the FBI plays in achieving the monetary results reflected in the HCFAC annual report and because that statute states that the funds are for the same purposes as the funds provided for HHS and DOJ under the Social Security Act, even though FBI spending and monetary results are not required to be reported, per the statute.

- While all mandatory HCFAC Account funding is included in the ROI calculation of this report, only certain portions of discretionary HCFAC funding is included. All discretionary HCFAC funding for HHS/OIG and DOJ are included in the HCFAC report ROI since they spend their discretionary funding on the same types of activities that they support with mandatory funding. Only the portion of CMS Medicare discretionary HCFAC funding that supports law enforcement is included in the HCFAC report ROI. The remainder of CMS's HCFAC Medicare discretionary funding supports activities in the Medicare Integrity Program (MIP) that are included in the MIP ROI, which is calculated separately and outside of the HCFAC report. All discretionary Medicaid Integrity program funding is included in a separate Medicaid Integrity program ROI published in a separate report.

GLOSSARY OF TERMS

The Account	The Health Care Fraud and Abuse Control Account
ACA	Affordable Care Act
AKS	Anti-Kickback Statute
AoA	Department of Health and Human Services, Administration on Aging
ASPA	Assistant Secretary for Public Affairs (HHS)
AUSA	Assistant United States Attorney
CHIP	Children's Health Insurance Program
CIA	Corporate Integrity Agreement
CMP	Civil Monetary Penalty
CMS	Department of Health and Human Services, Centers for Medicare & Medicaid Services

CNC	Compromised Number Contractors
CPI	Center Program Integrity
CPI-U	Consumer Price Index – Urban Consumers
CRIPA	Civil Rights of Institutionalized Persons Act
CY	Calendar Year
DAB	Department of Health and Human Services, Departmental Appeals Board
DEA	Drug Enforcement Administration
DME	Durable Medical Equipment
DMEPOS	Durable Medical Equipment Prosthetics, Orthotics, and Supplies
DOJ	The Department of Justice
DPA	Deferred Prosecution Agreement
DRA	Deficit Reduction Act of 2005
EOUSA	Executive Office for the United States Attorneys
FEHBP	Federal Employee Health Benefits Program
FBI	Federal Bureau of Investigation
FCA	False Claims Act
FDA	Food and Drug Administration
FDCA	Food, Drug, and Cosmetic Act
FI	Fiscal Intermediaries
FLI	Fraud Level Indicator
FY	Fiscal Year
HCFAC	Health Care Fraud and Abuse Control Program or the Program
HEAT	Health Care Fraud Prevention & Enforcement Action Team
HHA	Home Health Agency
HHS	The Department of Health and Human Services
HHS/OIG	The Department of Health and Human Services – Office of the Inspector General
HI	Hospital Insurance Trust Fund
HIPAA, or the Act	The Health Insurance Portability and Accountability Act of 1996, P.L. 104-191
HIV	Human Immunodeficiency Virus
IPIA	Improper Payments Information Act of 2002, P.L. 107-300
MEDIC	Medicare Drug Integrity Contractors MFCU – Medicaid Fraud Control Unit

OCRS	Organized Crime and Racketeering Section
OGC	Office of the General Counsel, Department of Health and Human Services
PDE	Prescription Drug Event
PERM	Program Error Rate Measurement
PFPP	Pharmaceutical Fraud Pilot Program
The Program	The Health Care Fraud and Abuse Control Program
Secretary	The Secretary of the Department of Health and Human Services
SMP	Senior Medicare Patrol
TRHCA	Tax Relief and Health Care Act
USAO	United States Attorney's Office
ZPIC	Zone Program Integrity Contractor

End Notes

[1] Hereafter, referred to as the Secretary.

[2] The amount reported as won or negotiated only reflects Federal recoveries and therefore does not reflect state Medicaid monies recovered as part of any global, Federal-State settlements.

[3] Also known as the Medicare Hospital Insurance (Part A) Trust Fund and the Supplemental Medical Insurance (Part B) Trust Fund.

[4] The CPI-U adjustment in TRHCA did not apply to the Medicare Integrity Program (MIP).

[5] In FY 2007, mandatory funds became available until expended. Discretionary funding is two-year funding.

[6] In addition, HHS/OIG obligated $11.3 million in funds received as "reimbursement for the costs of conducting investigations and audits and for monitoring compliance plans" as authorized by section 1128C(b) of the Social Security Act, 42 U.S.C. § 1320a-7c(b).

[7] In addition, in FY 2011, the FBI received $128.4 million in mandatory HIPAA funding.

[8] Amounts only represent those that are provided by statute, and do not include other mandatory sources or discretionary appropriated sources provided through Departments' annual appropriations.

[9] Note that some of the judgments, settlements, and administrative actions that occurred in FY 2011 will result in transfers in future years, just as some of the transfers in FY 2011 are attributable to actions from prior years.

[10] HHS collected approximately $428.1 million in HHS/OIG recommended recoveries which are included in the total $2.5 billion transferred to the Trust Funds in FY 2011 and to the Treasury.

[11] The accomplishments figures presented in the bullets include all reported Strike Force cases handled by DOJ Criminal Division attorneys and AUSAs in the respective USAOs during FY 2011.

[12] These statistics are for the period of May 7, 2007 through September 30, 2011.

[13] In addition to the funds made available to OIG from the HCFAC account under HIPAA, Congress has provided funds to OIG specifically for oversight of the Medicaid program.

The Deficit Reduction Act of 2005 (DRA, P.L. 109-171), the Supplemental Appropriations Act of 2008 (Pub. L. 110-252) at § 7001(b), and the American Recovery and Reinvestment Act of 2009 (Pub. L. 111-5) at § 5007(b) each appropriated funding for Medicaid-related oversight efforts. Therefore, OIG's Medicaid activities cited throughout this report may have drawn from these funding sources, in addition to HCFAC.

[14] When a USAO accepts a criminal referral for consideration, the office opens it as a matter pending in the district. A referral remains a pending matter until an indictment or information is filed or it is declined for prosecution.

[15] Fraud Section attorneys litigated 11 of the 17 Medicare Fraud Strike Force trials during FY 2010. Several of these trials were summarized previously in the "Medicare Fraud Strike Force" section of this report.

[16] The U.S. Attorney's Office for the Northern District of Illinois implemented the Strike Force in Chicago and is providing management and oversight for Strike Force prosecutions in that district.

In: The Health Care Fraud and Abuse Program ISBN: 978-1-62417-425-4
Editor: Lorena Townsend

Chapter 2

HEALTH CARE FRAUD AND ABUSE CONTROL PROGRAM: IMPROVEMENTS NEEDED IN CONTROLS OVER REPORTING DEPOSITS AND EXPENDITURES*

United States Government Accountability Office

ABBREVIATIONS

AEM	ASPEN Enforcement Manager
CMS	Centers for Medicare & Medicaid Services
CPI-U	consumer price index for all urban consumers
FACS	Financial Accounting and Control System
DOJ	Department of Justice
HCFAC	Health Care Fraud and Abuse Control program
HEAT	Health Care Fraud Prevention and Enforcement Action Team
HHS	Department of Health and Human Services
HI	Hospital Insurance

* This is an edited, reformatted and augmented version of The United States Government Accountability Office publication, Report to the Ranking Member, Committee on the Judiciary, U.S. Senate, GAO-11-446, dated May 2011.

HIPAA	Health Insurance Portability and Accountability Act
IPAC	Intra-governmental Payment and Collection System
OIG	Office of Inspector General
OMB	Office of Management and Budget
SMI	Supplementary Medical Insurance
TRHCA	Tax Relief and Health Care Act
USAO	United States Attorneys Office

Why GAO Did This Study

To help combat fraud and abuse in health care programs, including Medicare and Medicaid, Congress enacted the Health Care Fraud and Abuse Control (HCFAC) program as part of the Health Insurance Portability and Accountability Act of 1996 (HIPAA).

HIPAA requires that the Departments of Health and Human Services (HHS) and Justice (DOJ) issue a joint annual report to Congress on amounts deposited to and appropriated from the Federal Hospital Insurance (HI) Trust Fund for the HCFAC program.

In April 2005, GAO reported on the results of its review of HCFAC program activities for fiscal years 2002 and 2003 and made recommendations to HHS and DOJ.

The objectives of this requested review were to assess the extent to which HHS and DOJ (1) took actions to address the recommendations made in the 2005 report and (2) designed effective controls over reporting HCFAC deposits and expenditures for fiscal years 2008 and 2009. GAO reviewed HHS and DOJ documentation; selected nongeneralizable samples; and interviewed agency officials.

What GAO Recommends

GAO makes 11 recommendations to HHS and DOJ to revise or develop written procedures that include documentation and monitoring controls for HCFAC activities and reporting. DOJ agreed with all four of its recommendations.

Of the seven recommendations to HHS, it generally agreed with five, disagreed with one, and did not address the remaining recommendation.

What GAO Found

Although HHS and DOJ have taken action to address our previous recommendations aimed at improving procedures for recording HCFAC expenditures and issuing the annual HCFAC report, GAO found that controls are not sufficient to ensure that the report is accurate and supported. HHS and DOJ took action to address three of the four recommendations in GAO's 2005 report related to recording staff hours in agency workload tracking systems, using the appropriate account class to record HCFAC expenditure data, and expediting the review process for issuing the annual HCFAC report. Neither agency agreed with the remaining recommendation to notify Congress on delays in issuing the HCFAC report within 1 month after missing the mandated January 1 deadline and thus, did not take action. However, in June 2010, HHS and DOJ implemented an expedited review process for completing the HCFAC report. The fiscal year 2010 HCFAC report was issued on January 24, 2011, 23 days later than the mandated reporting date. According to DOJ officials responsible for preparing the HCFAC report, they intend to use this new expedited review process to meet the mandated deadline when preparing future year reports.

Regarding the design of controls, while HHS and DOJ had designed polices and procedures for documentation that generally required the retention of documentation for 6 years, these did not provide sufficient controls to ensure adequate support of HCFAC deposits and expenditures, in accordance with internal control standards.

- Components at both HHS and DOJ that manage HCFAC activities did not include in their respective policies and procedures controls that specified the person responsible for maintaining the records, the location of records, or a combination of both.
- GAO found instances at HHS and DOJ where documentation could not be provided to support HCFAC expenditures, such as time and attendance reports.

Also, both agencies did not have sufficient monitoring controls such as reconciliations, comparisons, and supervisory reviews, as outlined in internal control standards, to ensure accurate reporting of HCFAC deposits and expenditures. As a result, GAO found instances where data recorded in accounting and payroll systems were inconsistent with other sources such as the HI trust fund statements and agency workload tracking systems. GAO also identified presentation errors in the 2008 and 2009 annual HCFAC reports. For example, in reviewing the line item for restitution and compensatory damages, GAO found that $717 million (70 percent) of the $1.03 billion reported in the fiscal year 2009 HCFAC report was not transferred to the HI trust fund as stated in the report. These amounts, primarily related to Medicare Part B and Medicaid, were transferred to the Federal Supplementary Medical Insurance Trust Fund and the Medicaid appropriation account as required. These inaccuracies overstated the amount of funds transferred to the HI trust fund.

May 10, 2011

The Honorable Charles E. Grassley
Ranking Member
Committee on the Judiciary
United States Senate

Dear Senator Grassley:

We have designated Medicare and Medicaid as high risk programs because they are particularly vulnerable to fraud, waste, and abuse and improper payments.[1] Medicare is considered high risk in part because of its complexity and susceptibility to improper payments, and Medicaid because of concerns about the adequacy of its fiscal oversight to prevent inappropriate spending. In 2010, Medicare covered 47 million elderly and disabled beneficiaries and had estimated outlays of $509 billion. Medicaid, a federal-state program, covered over 69 million low-income people and consists of more than 50 distinct state-based programs that cost the federal government and states an estimated $408 billion in fiscal year 2010. For fiscal year 2010, the Department of Health and Human Services (HHS) estimated improper payments for the Medicare and Medicaid programs at about $70.4 billion,[2] comprising 56 percent of the estimated $125.4 billion in governmentwide improper payments, as reported by federal agencies.[3]

To help combat fraud and abuse in health care programs such as Medicare and Medicaid, Congress enacted the Health Care Fraud and Abuse Control (HCFAC) program as part of the Health Insurance Portability and Accountability Act of 1996 (HIPAA).[4] HHS and the Department of Justice (DOJ) jointly administer the HCFAC program. HIPAA requires that HHS and DOJ issue a joint annual report to Congress no later than January 1 of each year on (1) amounts deposited to the Federal Hospital Insurance Trust Fund

(HI trust fund) pursuant to HIPAA (HCFAC deposits) for the previous fiscal year and the source of such amounts and (2) amounts appropriated from the HI trust fund for HCFAC activities each year and the justification for the expenditure of such amounts.[5]

In April 2005, we reported on the results of our review of HCFAC-related activities for fiscal years 2002 and 2003.[6] In that report, we made recommendations to HHS and DOJ to improve procedures for recording HCFAC expenditures and issuing the annual HCFAC report. You requested that we provide an update on the status of the recommendations in our April 2005 report and review controls over the reporting process for amounts included in the fiscal years 2008 and 2009 HCFAC reports.[7] As agreed with your office, the objectives of our review were to assess the extent to which HHS and DOJ (1) took actions to address the recommendations we made in 2005 and (2) designed effective controls over reporting HCFAC deposits and expenditures for fiscal years 2008 and 2009.

To address the first objective, we reviewed supporting documentation provided by HHS and DOJ such as policies and procedures and interviewed officials at HHS and DOJ, including the HHS Acting Deputy Inspector General and the Assistant Director of the Executive Office for United States Attorneys, to obtain further information on actions taken. To address the second objective, we obtained and reviewed relevant HHS and DOJ policies and procedures for reporting deposits and expenditures within each agency and used criteria outlined in our *Standards for Internal Control in the Federal Government* to assess the effectiveness of the controls documented in these policies and procedures.[8] To further our understanding of these controls, we selected a nongeneralizable stratified random sample for deposits of 47 transactions for fiscal year 2008 and 55 transactions for fiscal year 2009. We also selected a nongeneralizable random sample for expenditures of 63 transactions for fiscal year 2008 and 62 transactions for fiscal year 2009. Expenditure samples were selected for each of the agency components that were allocated HCFAC appropriation funds as reported in the annual HCFAC reports for fiscal years 2008 and 2009. The sample selections were designed to provide additional details about the processing of those transactions and were not intended to be representative of the universe of HCFAC transactions. For the selected transactions, we reviewed supporting documentation such as check registers, time and attendance reports, and contracts to determine whether dollar amounts for these transactions were accurately reported and the use of funds were consistent with HIPAA. We also performed additional procedures for HHS Office of Inspector General (OIG) payroll transactions to determine if HCFAC projects were properly classified and workload tracking systems included hours for all staff. In addition, we conducted interviews with HHS and DOJ officials including budget analysts and financial specialists to obtain an understanding and clarification of the processes in place to report HCFAC deposits and expenditures. See appendix I for additional details on our objectives, scope, and methodology.

We conducted our work from February 2010 through May 2011 in accordance with U.S. generally accepted government auditing standards. Those standards require that we plan and perform the audit to obtain sufficient, appropriate evidence to provide a reasonable basis for our findings and conclusions based on our audit objectives. We believe that the evidence obtained provides a reasonable basis for our findings and conclusions based on our audit objectives.

BACKGROUND

HIPAA authorized the HCFAC program to consolidate and strengthen ongoing efforts to combat fraud and abuse in health care programs and increase resources for fighting health care fraud. The Secretary of HHS, through the HHS OIG, and the Attorney General, administer the HCFAC program. The HCFAC program goals are to:

- coordinate federal, state, and local law enforcement efforts to control fraud and abuse associated with health plans;
- conduct investigations, audits, and other studies of delivery and payment for health care for the United States;
- facilitate the enforcement of the civil, criminal, and administrative statutes applicable to health care;
- provide guidance to the health care industry, including the issuance of advisory opinions, safe harbor notices, and special fraud alerts; and
- establish a national database of adverse actions against health care providers.

Figure 1 below provides an overview of the HCFAC funding stream, including the related deposits, the allocation of appropriated funds to carry out federal health care law enforcement activities, and the reporting mandate.

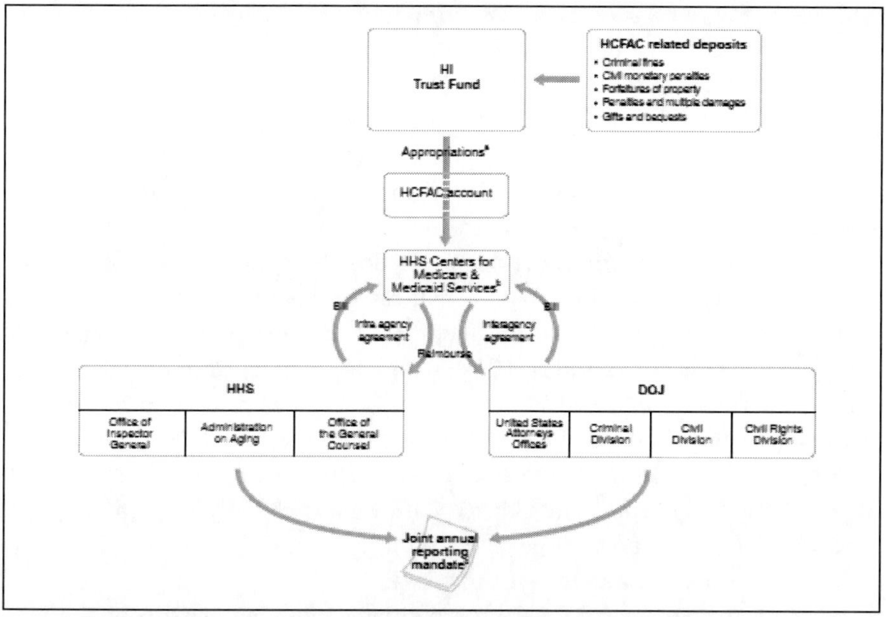

Source: GAO analysis of HIPAA legislation and HHS and DOJ data.

[a] The annual appropriated amount is allocated between the various HHS and DOJ components based on statutory amounts and internal negotiations. An allocation is made when one or more agencies share the administration of the program for which appropriations are made to only one of the agencies or to the President. The agency receiving the allocation may obligate up to the amount included in the account.

[b] HHS's Centers for Medicare & Medicaid Services (CMS), Division of Accounting Operations, performs the accounting for the HCFAC account.

[c] HIPAA requires that HHS and DOJ issue a joint annual report to Congress no later than January 1 of each year that identifies the amounts appropriated to and from the HI trust fund during the prior fiscal year.

Figure 1. Overview of HCFAC Funding Stream.

The types of collections deposited to the HI trust fund and appropriations from this fund, including related expenditures are discussed below.

Deposits to the HI Trust Fund

Criminal fines. DOJ prosecutes entities or persons that are involved in commission of a federal health care offense, such as mail fraud related to a health care program.[9] Courts assess criminal fines upon which the criminal debtor is ordered to submit payment(s) to the United States District Court where the case was prosecuted. Each District Court coordinates with DOJ's local United States Attorneys Office (USAO)[10] to communicate collections received.[11] The Executive Office for United States Attorneys report collection data on a quarterly basis to the Bureau of the Public Debt for deposit into the HI trust fund.[12]

Civil monetary penalties. The Social Security Act authorizes the Secretary of HHS to impose civil monetary penalties for improper claims and other violations by health care providers, facilities, and other parties.[13] Centers for Medicare & Medicaid Services (CMS) regional offices impose some civil monetary penalties. CMS's Office of Financial Management collects the civil monetary penalties imposed on behalf of the Secretary of HHS and allocates payments received based on information the regional offices record in their data collection system. The Office of Financial Management reports collections for civil monetary penalties on a daily basis to the Bureau of the Public Debt for deposit into the HI trust fund.

Forfeitures of property. DOJ prosecutions of entities or persons that are involved in a federal health care offense can result in the forfeiture of property.[14] HHS and DOJ reported no property forfeitures creditable to the HI trust fund under HIPAA in the HCFAC reports for fiscal years 2008 and 2009.[15]

Penalties and multiple damages. Courts can impose penalties and multiple damages as a result of HHS and DOJ civil suits against those who have knowingly made false health care claims against the government, such as submitting claims for medical services that were not provided.[16] Of all civil debt collections received, DOJ is entitled to keep 3 percent in its Working Capital Fund for expenses incurred in processing and tracking civil and criminal debt collection litigations.[17] Both CMS and DOJ report collections for penalties and multiple damages on a continuous basis to the Bureau of the Public Debt for deposit into the HI trust fund.

Gifts and bequests. CMS occasionally receives gifts and bequests and equally splits the amount received between its Medicare Part A and Medicare Part B programs.[18] Gifts and bequests are donations received from individuals or entities, usually in the form of checks. Upon receipt of a donation, CMS records the amount in its accounting system and reports it to the Bureau of the Public Debt for deposit into the HI trust fund.

In addition to the types of deposits authorized by HIPAA and discussed above, HHS and DOJ report other types of collections in connection with health care fraud activities such as HHS OIG audit disallowances and court-awarded restitution and compensatory damages.[19] These types of collections represent amounts recovered by HHS and DOJ as a result of health care enforcement activities. These amounts are returned to the HI trust fund to the extent that they represent repayments to Medicare.[20]

Appropriations from the HI Trust Fund and Related Expenditures

Funds for the HCFAC program are appropriated from the HI trust fund to an expenditure account, referred to as the Health Care Fraud and Abuse Control Account (HCFAC account) maintained within the HI trust fund. Annually, the HHS Secretary and the Attorney General jointly certify amounts appropriated from the HI trust fund to the HCFAC account as necessary to finance health care fraud and abuse control activities based on statutory limits. HIPAA, as amended, prescribes the maximum amount that may be certified in a given fiscal year.[21] Any unexpended amounts are carried forward to the next fiscal year. Once HCFAC funds have been certified, CMS's Division of Accounting Operations performs the accounting for appropriations transferred to the HCFAC account. CMS makes funds available by creating allotments in its accounting system to fund related HCFAC expenditures.[22] CMS provides funds to other HHS components and DOJ through intra- and interagency agreements, as shown in figure 1. This process requires HHS and DOJ to bill CMS through the Intra-governmental Payment and Collection (IPAC) System to obtain payment from their allocation of HCFAC funds.[23] In addition to CMS's central accounting for HFCAC funds, both HHS and DOJ components have processes to separately manage their allotted HCFAC amounts. In general, these processes include authorizing HCFAC-related expenditures, recording applicable payroll and nonpayroll expenditures incurred to a designated HCFAC code, and reporting any unexpended amounts to be carried forward to the next fiscal year.

For fiscal year 2009, the Secretary of HHS and the Attorney General certified $266.4 million in mandatory funding to be appropriated from the HI trust fund to the HCFAC account.[24] Additionally, Congress appropriated $198 million in discretionary funding to that account in response to HHS's fiscal year 2009 budget request, to fund HCFAC program integrity activities. As such, the total appropriated amount to the HCFAC account for fiscal year 2009 was $464.4 million for that year.[25] Figure 2 provides a historical trend of the amounts appropriated to the HCFAC account over the past 13 fiscal years.

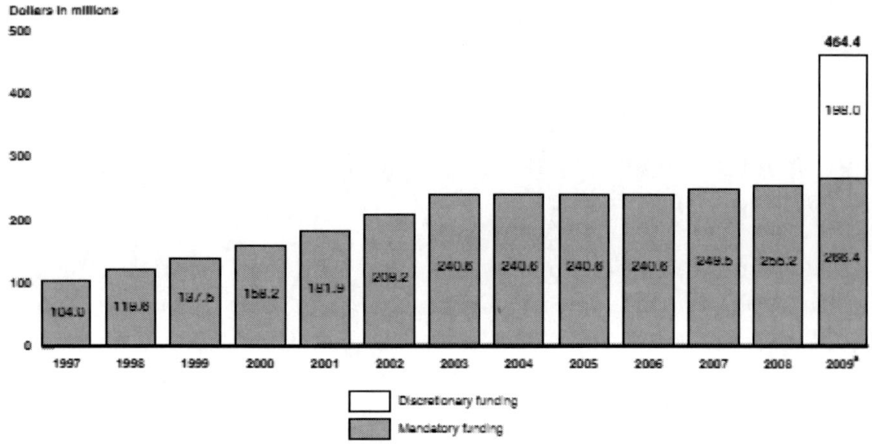

Source: The annual joint HHS and DOJ HCFAC reports for fiscal years 1997 through 2009.

[a] Fiscal year 2009 was the first year that Congress appropriated discretionary funding to the HCFAC account to support health care fraud and abuse activities. The Omnibus Appropriations Act of 2009 (Pub. L. No. 111-8) appropriated $198 million out of the HI and Federal Supplementary Medical Insurance (SMI) trust funds to HCFAC.

Figure 2. Amounts Appropriated for HCFAC, Fiscal Years 1997 through 2009.

Funds were first appropriated to HCFAC in fiscal year 1997. HIPAA limited the amounts appropriated for fiscal years 1998 through 2003 to an amount equal to the limit for the preceding fiscal year plus an additional 15 percent. For fiscal years 2004 through 2006, the amount made available was capped at the 2003 limit. The Tax Relief and Health Care Act (TRHCA) also allowed for yearly increases to the HCFAC account based on the change in the consumer price index for all urban consumers (CPI-U) over the previous fiscal year for fiscal years 2007 through 2010. In fiscal year 2006, TRHCA amended HIPAA so that funds allotted from the HCFAC account are available until expended.[26] Beyond 2010, the Patient Protection and Affordable Care Act,27 as amended by the Health Care and Education Reconciliation Act of 2010,28 raised the limit on funds that may be certified for the HCFAC account by the Secretary of HHS and the Attorney General by an additional $350 million over the next 10 years, beginning in fiscal year 2011.

The annual allocation of appropriation amounts to the HHS and DOJ components are intended to support a variety of anti-fraud and anti-abuse activities. For example, in May 2009, HHS and DOJ established a task force—the Health Care Fraud Prevention and Enforcement Action Team (HEAT)—comprised of top level law enforcement and professional staff from both agencies to prevent health care fraud and enforce current antifraud laws around the country. Other examples include HHS OIG investigations, audits, and evaluations that identify vulnerabilities for questionable or fraudulent financial practices related to Medicaid outpatient prescription drug expenditures and Medicare contractor costs. Similarly, DOJ's USAOs use HCFAC funding to support civil and criminal health care fraud and abuse litigation. HCFAC funds are also used to train attorneys, investigators, and auditors in the investigation and prosecution of health care fraud and abuse; prosecute health care matters through criminal, civil, and administrative proceedings; and conduct investigations, financial, and performance audits of health care programs, inspections, and other evaluations.

AGENCIES TOOK ACTION TO ADDRESS THREE OF FOUR GAO RECOMMENDATIONS

In our April 2005 report,[29] we identified weaknesses related to not properly capturing certain expenditure data in agency information systems, nonadherence to accounting policy for select HCFAC expenditures, and lengthy HCFAC report review processes. We made recommendations to HHS and DOJ to improve procedures for recording HCFAC expenditures and issuing the annual HCFAC report.[30] Based on our analysis of documentation, HHS and DOJ took actions that addressed three of the four recommendations. Both agencies disagreed with our recommendation to notify Congress on delays in issuing the HCFAC report by the mandated deadline and thus, did not take action. Each of the recommendations and applicable actions taken are described further below.

Record staff hours in workload tracking systems. In our 2005 report, we found that two HHS OIG components—Office of Evaluations and Inspections and Office of Investigations—had not recorded all staff hours in their workload tracking systems, which are used to monitor actual hours spent on HCFAC activities. HHS OIG uses the workload tracking systems to monitor HCFAC payroll expenditures, and incomplete information could hinder those efforts. We recommended that the HHS Inspector General require all HHS OIG components to develop procedures for ensuring that all key staff hours spent on HCFAC activities are recorded in the HHS OIG workload tracking systems. In April 2006, the HHS OIG's Office of Evaluation and Inspections updated its procedures for entering information into its workload tracking system, including guidance related to the completion of timesheets. The procedures instruct employees to record time to specific inspection codes and instruct managers to review staff time recorded in the system. In addition, HHS OIG's Office of Investigations updated its procedures in October 2009, which require all Office of Investigations personnel to record time and attendance in its workload tracking system. We determined that HHS OIG components' actions substantially addressed the recommendation.

Record expenditure data under the correct account class. In our 2005 report, we noted that only one of the four DOJ components receiving HCFAC funds properly recorded expenditures as required by DOJ policies and procedures. We recommended that the Attorney General develop monitoring procedures to ensure that DOJ components record key HCFAC program expenditure data under the appropriate HCFAC account class in DOJ's accounting system. In April 2005, DOJ updated its policies and procedures that require individual components to monitor obligations recorded in the accounting system on a quarterly basis. Further, in fiscal year 2009 the Executive Office for the United States Attorneys provided procedures to the USAOs, which receive the largest portion of the HCFAC allocation, on how to charge HCFAC expenditures using the proper program code. According to DOJ officials, component officials review system reports on a regular basis to verify that HCFAC obligations and expenditures are correctly reflected in the accounting system. We determined that DOJ's actions were sufficient to close the recommendation.

Develop a more expedited review process. In our 2005 report, we noted that a lengthy review process within HHS and DOJ resulted in failure to meet the mandated annual January 1 deadline for reporting HCFAC activities. For example, the fiscal year 2003 HCFAC report, the most recent report at the time of that review, was issued 1 year after the mandated reporting date. We recommended that the Secretary of HHS and the Attorney General develop a more expedited review process for the joint annual HCFAC reports. In June 2010, DOJ issued a *Report Completion Guide*, an expedited review process that provides instructions and time frames for submitting information to complete the annual HCFAC report. The guide introduced a new process whereby DOJ and HHS components utilized a shared website to distribute documents for edit and review. The guide also established time frames for issuing the fiscal year 2010 HCFAC report by January 1, 2011. Using these new time frames, HHS and DOJ jointly issued the fiscal year 2010 HCFAC report on January 24, 2011, only 23 days later than the mandated reporting date. According to DOJ officials responsible for preparing the HCFAC report, they intend to use these time frames to meet the mandated deadline when preparing future year reports. We determined that HHS and DOJ's efforts meet the intent of our recommendation. However, as discussed later in this report, although timeliness is important, ensuring that the report is accurate and reliable remains a concern.

Notify Congress of delays in report issuance. In our 2005 report, we noted that repeated delays in issuing the joint annual HCFAC report impact the relevance of the data being reported. We recommended that the Secretary of HHS and the Attorney General notify congressional oversight committees of delays in issuing the annual report within 1 month of missing the January 1 deadline. HHS and DOJ did not concur with this recommendation. However, as we stated above, both HHS and DOJ developed and implemented a new timeline of dates to edit and review the annual HCFAC report, which resulted in issuing the fiscal year 2010 annual HCFAC report within one month of the mandate. Continuing to take steps to meet these internal deadlines will be necessary to issue the HCFAC report by the mandated deadline to provide timely, relevant information to Congress.

HHS AND DOJ HAVE GAPS IN DOCUMENTATION AND MONITORING CONTROLS OVER REPORTING HCFAC DEPOSITS AND EXPENDITURES

Our review of HHS and DOJ policies and procedures showed that both agencies had not designed sufficient controls to help ensure that HCFAC deposits and expenditures were accurately reported. GAO's *Standards for Internal Control in the Federal Government* provides that management should establish control mechanisms and activities, and monitor and evaluate these controls. Specifically, during our review we found that HHS and DOJ did not have sufficient controls in their policies and procedures with respect to (1) maintaining and retaining supporting documentation for HCFAC deposits and expenditures and (2) monitoring HCFAC deposits and expenditures to help ensure accurate reporting. From our review of the underlying documentation to support HCFAC activities and nongeneralizable samples of deposits and expenditures, we identified instances in which these design deficiencies resulted in HHS's and DOJ's inability to support reported amounts for HCFAC expenditures. We also found errors in reported HCFAC amounts.[31]

Documentation Controls Insufficient to Fully Support HCFAC Deposits and Expenditures

While HHS and DOJ designed controls that were incorporated into its policies and procedures generally requiring the retention of documentation for 6 years, the policies and procedures for CMS, Administration on Aging, and DOJ did not provide sufficient details with respect to where these documents were to be filed, who should be responsible for maintaining them, or a combination of both, which would help ensure accountability and adequate support of HCFAC deposits and expenditures.

Our review found that while the HHS OIG and the Office of the General Counsel policies and procedures for documentation contained sufficient controls as to the type of documentation to be retained, the retention period, the location of records, and the person responsible for maintaining the records, CMS and Administration on Aging policies and procedures were lacking some of these controls.[32]

Specifically, CMS policies and procedures for documentation of HCFAC deposits and expenditures, did not identify the person responsible for maintaining supporting documents. We found the same weakness with Administration on Aging policies and procedures for documentation of HCFAC expenditures.

Further, Administration on Aging policies and procedures did not specify where those documents should be filed.

Officials from the Administration on Aging told us that they are in the process of revising their policies and procedures to address these issues. In its comments, Administration on Aging indicated that it expects to incorporate these changes by summer 2011.

We also reviewed DOJ's controls for retention of documents related to HCFAC deposits and expenditures.[33] DOJ's procedures for deposits identified controls related to the type of documentation to be retained, the retention period, and the location of records, but they did not specify the person responsible for maintaining supporting documents. Although DOJ's departmentwide expenditure procedures identified controls related to the type of documentation and the retention period, and indicated that documents should be maintained in the obligation file, the procedures did not specify the location of the obligation file and the person responsible for maintaining the records within each office.

During our review, we found instances at HHS and DOJ where documentation was not available to support expenditures. For example, we found that HHS's Administration on Aging did not maintain, and therefore could not provide, underlying documentation to support how the estimated payroll percentages for fiscal years 2008 and 2009 were derived, which are used to charge payroll expenditures against the HCFAC account on a biweekly basis.

In fiscal year 2008, for example, the Administration on Aging charged approximately 29 percent of its total HCFAC allocation, or $879,607, to payroll expenses, an amount that could not be fully supported due to the lack of documentation. Therefore, we were unable to verify the justification of such expenditures. In addition, during our review, we found that DOJ could not provide sufficient documentation to support 12 nongeneralizable payroll sample items selected for fiscal years 2008 and 2009, such as time and attendance reports, workload tracking system reports, and records of actual payroll disbursements.

Further, DOJ could not provide documentation to support unexpended amounts carried forward from fiscal year 2008 to fiscal year 2009, totaling $522,278. At the end of each fiscal year, DOJ communicates to HHS the amount of unused funds so that HHS can carry them forward to the following fiscal year via an interagency agreement. To report this amount, DOJ's Justice Management Division compiles obligation data provided by the different DOJ components. However, DOJ's Justice Management Division could not locate the documents that supported the amount of funds carried forward in the fiscal year 2009 interagency agreement.

GAO's Standards for Internal Control in the Federal Government provides that internal control be designed to ensure that all transactions and other significant events be clearly documented and the documentation be readily available for examination.[34]

The standards also provide that records should be properly managed and maintained and documentation should appear in management directives, administrative policies, or operating manuals. Insufficient controls over documentation increase the risk of not having sufficient support to ensure reported HCFAC amounts are accurate and funds are spent as intended.

Monitoring Controls Insufficient to Help Ensure Accurate Reporting of HCFAC Deposits and Expenditures

HHS's and DOJ's procedures did not incorporate sufficient monitoring controls to help ensure HCFAC deposits and expenditures were accurately reported.

Monitoring of deposits. HHS and DOJ had not designed controls to require the reconciliation of HCFAC deposits recorded in their departmentwide accounting systems to data collection systems or to the HI trust fund statements.[35] Specifically, CMS did not have written procedures that required the reconciliation of civil monetary penalty amounts in the CMS regional offices' data collection system to CMS's accounting system.[36] We found two instances from our fiscal year 2009 nongeneralizable sample of deposits where CMS regional offices had made adjustments that were recorded in their data collection system, but not communicated to the Office of Financial Management for recording in CMS's accounting system, which is used as a source to compile the data for the HCFAC report. These two instances resulted in a $15,066 overstatement error in CMS's accounting system, which CMS officials corrected after we brought the errors to their attention. Although CMS officials stated that they reconcile the data maintained in both systems on a monthly basis, they were not able to provide us an example of these reconciliation reports. In February 2011, CMS officials told us that they were in the process of developing procedures for the Office of Financial Management to require these reconciliations.

In addition, DOJ's Justice Management Division[37] did not have written procedures that included controls to reconcile deposits of the 3 percent portion of penalties and multiple damages reported in the HI trust fund statements to the agency's accounting system records.[38] For example, for fiscal year 2009 we identified an overstatement in the amount of $596,266 in the HI trust fund statements when comparing to DOJ's records. When we inquired about the difference, DOJ officials from the Justice Management Division confirmed that an overstatement had occurred because of adjusting entries that had been communicated to the Bureau of the Public Debt but not captured in the HI trust fund statements. In February 2011, DOJ officials told us that to avoid this from happening in the future, they were in the process of developing procedures that would include monitoring controls for reconciling on a quarterly basis penalties and multiple damages between DOJ records and the statements issued by the Bureau of the Public Debt to ensure reported amounts are accurate and consistent between both agencies.

Monitoring of expenditures. Similarly, certain HHS components and DOJ did not have written procedures that incorporated controls for reconciling or comparing HCFAC staff hours to verify the accuracy of payroll expenditures charged against the HCFAC account. Specifically, HHS's Administration on Aging did not have controls for monitoring HCFAC actual payroll hours. HHS's Administration on Aging charges payroll expenditures based on estimates made prior to or after the beginning of the year. Because the Administration on Aging does not record hours at the HCFAC activity level, it cannot verify that the payroll expenditures charged against the HCFAC account throughout the year are reasonably accurate. According to officials at the Administration on Aging, they believe that tracking hours at the HCFAC activity level would not be cost effective nor provide better results to justify the costs. However, because the estimated percentage of time charged against the HCFAC account may not represent the actual time spent on HCFAC activities for a given pay period, it is critical that some type of monitoring procedures or verification procedures are designed to help ensure that the payroll expenditures charged to the HCFAC account are reasonable and supported. DOJ's Civil Rights Division also charges HCFAC payroll expenditures based on estimates. Although Civil Rights Division officials indicated that they track and record actual hours and make adjustments to payroll expenditures if differences are noted, these controls were not documented in DOJ's policies and procedures.

In addition, HHS OIG and the Office of the General Counsel for HHS, as well as DOJ USAO and Civil Division, did not have written procedures that included controls for reconciling or comparing HCFAC hours recorded in workload tracking systems to departmentwide payroll or accounting systems. We found instances where staff hours captured in workload tracking systems did not agree with staff hours recorded in departmentwide payroll or accounting systems. For example, we found that the workload tracking system used by the Office of Counsel to the Inspector General included approximately 10 percent fewer hours for fiscal year 2008 and 7 percent fewer hours in fiscal year 2009 when compared to HHS's payroll system reports. Similarly, we found two instances from our fiscal year 2008 nongeneralizable sample of expenditures where USAO's workload tracking system included fewer hours than the HCFAC hours recorded and billed in DOJ's accounting system, which collectively accounted for a 40 percent difference between the two systems. Failure to complete these reconciliations or comparisons could lead to unsubstantiated payroll expenditures that should not be charged to the HCFAC account.[39] HHS OIG and DOJ officials told us that they were aware of the differences. HHS OIG officials indicated that while they did not have procedures that specifically addressed the reconciliation of data captured in their workload tracking systems, they believed they had other compensating controls, such as periodic inspections of timesheets, to mitigate the risk of inconsistent data between systems.

They also noted that they were considering taking actions to revise their policies and procedures to add new monitoring controls to address the need to reconcile data between the systems. Further, DOJ officials indicated that because they spend significantly more resources on HCFAC activities than the sum that is allocated to DOJ from the HCFAC account, it is not cost beneficial to require personnel to record their time consistently in both systems. Also, according to DOJ officials, although not formally documented, each component has processes to monitor HCFAC expenditures to ensure they do not over-bill the HCFAC account. For example, the officials stated that the Criminal Division performs quarterly reviews of percentages used to charge payroll expenditures against the HCFAC account. Not having policies and procedures to ensure that sufficient controls over HCFAC expenditures are in place could result in misstatements and ultimately hinder HHS and DOJ managers in preparing meaningful budgets to support future HCFAC funding requests.

Monitoring of annual report compilation. Also, we found that although DOJ issued the *Report Completion Guide* in June 2010 that specified time frames for both HHS and DOJ for submitting information to complete the annual HCFAC report, the guide did not require that monitoring control activities, such as comparisons and supervisory reviews, be performed to help ensure that reported amounts were accurately presented. During our review of the HCFAC reports, we found presentation errors of $245.7 million and $717.5 million for fiscal years 2008 and 2009, respectively, of the total amounts reported as transferred to the HI trust fund. For example, for fiscal year 2009 we found that $716.8 million of the $1.0 billion reported in the restitution and compensatory damages line item was not transferred to the HI trust fund as stated in the report.

Of the $716.8 million, $441.0 million related to Medicaid, $245.4 million related to Medicare Part B, and $30.4 million represented a double-counting error.

The $30.4 million double-counting error related to civil monetary penalties and CMS's portion of penalties and multiple damages, which were already reported under separate line items. HHS and DOJ disclosed the double-counting error and the Medicaid presentation error in the fiscal year

2010 annual HCFAC report issued on January 24, 2011. Recoveries for Medicare Part B and Medicaid are not transferred to the HI trust fund, but instead are to be transferred to the Federal Supplementary Medical Insurance (SMI) Trust Fund and the Medicaid appropriation account within CMS, respectively. We found a similar issue in the fiscal year 2008 HCFAC report, where the total amount reported as transferred to the HI trust fund included Medicare Part B recoveries totaling $245.7 million. These inaccuracies overstated the amount of funds transferred to the HI trust fund.

In addition, CMS officials told us that the amounts reported in the HHS OIG audit disallowances line item, totaling about $662.5 million and $360.2 million for fiscal years 2008 and 2009, respectively, included both Medicare and Medicaid recoveries.

As stated above, Medicaid recoveries are to be transferred to the Medicaid appropriation account within CMS rather than the HI trust fund. However, these officials stated that the dollar amount associated with each type of recovery could not be determined because the current system does not readily distinguish between Medicare and Medicaid recoveries for amounts previously reported in the HCFAC report. Full disclosures had not been made in the report to inform readers that reported amounts included Medicare Part B and Medicaid, which are not transferred to the HI trust fund. In the fiscal years 2008 and 2009 HCFAC reports, HHS and DOJ incorrectly indicated in footnotes that reported amounts did not include Medicaid funds. CMS officials indicated they will separately report Medicare and Medicaid recoveries related to HHS OIG audit disallowances in future HCFAC reports. According to CMS officials, they plan to accomplish this by manually tracking Medicare and Medicaid recoveries.

In addition, DOJ officials told us that they are in the process of developing written guidance on the preparation of the annual HCFAC report and anticipate issuance by June 2011.

GAO's Standards for Internal Control in the Federal Government provides that internal control should generally be designed to assure that ongoing monitoring occurs in the course of normal operations, including regular management and supervisory activities, comparisons, reconciliations, and other actions people take in performing their duties.[40]

Having detailed written policies and procedures that incorporate these key monitoring controls decreases the risk of reporting inaccurate HCFAC data that could be misleading to Congress when judging the success of the program.

CONCLUSION

Although HHS and DOJ have taken action to address our previous recommendations aimed at improving procedures for recording HCFAC expenditures and issuing the annual HCFAC report, we found that controls are not sufficient to ensure that the report is accurate and supported. As HHS and DOJ accelerate the reporting process in an attempt to complete the report by the January 1 mandated reporting deadline, it is important that they establish controls that are designed to provide complete, accurate, and reliable information in the annual HCFAC report. Based on our review of the fiscal years 2008 and 2009 HCFAC reports, HHS and DOJ do not have sufficient controls for maintaining and retaining documentation and performing monitoring such as reconciliation and review activities to ensure accurate and consistent reporting of HCFAC deposits and expenditures. These design weaknesses led to instances where documentation was not readily available and amounts included in the HCFAC reports contained errors. Until HHS and DOJ strengthen their controls for documenting and monitoring HCFAC reporting processes, their ability to provide Congress with an accurate and timely annual report of HCFAC activities will continue to be compromised. Inaccuracies in the mandated annual report limit its usefulness to congressional decision makers and other interested.

RECOMMENDATIONS FOR EXECUTIVE ACTION

We are making the following 11 recommendations to HHS and DOJ to improve controls over the accounting and reporting of HCFAC activities.

We recommend that the Secretary of HHS,

- direct the Administrator of CMS to
  - revise procedures for properly maintaining supporting documentation for HCFAC deposits and expenditures, to include specifying the titles of staff responsible for maintaining supporting documentation;
  - develop written procedures that incorporate monitoring controls for HCFAC deposit information recorded in the departmentwide accounting system, including reconciling the deposit data in this system to the regional offices' data collection system;

- direct the Assistant Secretary for Aging to:
    - revise the Administration on Aging's procedures for properly maintaining supporting documentation for HCFAC expenditures, to include specifying the titles of staff responsible for maintaining supporting documentation and the location of records;
    - develop written procedures that incorporate monitoring controls to verify that the payroll expenditures charged against HCFAC are reasonable and supported; and
- direct the Acting General Counsel to develop written procedures that incorporate monitoring controls for the Office of the General Counsel staff hours related to HCFAC activities captured in workload tracking systems, including the reconciliation to staff hours captured in the departmentwide payroll system; and
- develop written procedures in collaboration with DOJ that incorporate monitoring controls for preparing the joint annual HCFAC report to help ensure reported amounts are accurate.

We recommend that the HHS Inspector General develop written procedures that incorporate monitoring controls for HHS OIG staff hours related to HCFAC activities captured in workload tracking systems, including the reconciliation to staff hours captured in the departmentwide payroll system.

We recommend that the Attorney General direct the Deputy Assistant Attorney General / Controller to:

- revise procedures for properly maintaining supporting documentation for HCFAC deposits and expenditures, to include specifying the titles of staff responsible for maintaining supporting documentation and the location of records;
- develop written procedures that incorporate monitoring controls for reconciling HCFAC deposits of the 3 percent portion of penalties and multiple damages information recorded in the departmentwide accounting system to the HI trust fund statements;
- develop written procedures that incorporate monitoring controls to verify that the payroll expenditures charged against HCFAC are reasonable and supported; and

- develop written procedures in collaboration with HHS that incorporate monitoring controls for preparing the joint annual HCFAC report to help ensure reported amounts are accurate.

AGENCY COMMENTS AND OUR EVALUATION

We provided a draft of this report to HHS and DOJ for review and comment. DOJ indicated via e-mail that it agreed with the findings and the four recommendations we made to revise or develop written procedures that include documentation and monitoring controls for HCFAC activities and reporting.

While DOJ did not provide written comments, it provided technical comments, as did HHS, that we incorporated as appropriate. We made a total of 11 recommendations, 7 to HHS and 4 to DOJ.

Of the seven recommendations we made, in its written comments, HHS generally agreed with five, disagreed with one, and did not address the remaining recommendation.

Specifically, HHS agreed with our recommendation related to revising the Administration on Aging's procedures for properly maintaining supporting documentation for HCFAC expenditures and stated that it plans to incorporate these changes by summer 2011. Also, HHS agreed with our recommendation to develop written procedures for preparing the joint annual HCFAC report and indicated that it has begun to work with DOJ to improve the *Report Completion Guide*. In addition, HHS OIG agreed with our recommendation to develop written procedures that incorporate monitoring controls for staff hours related to HCFAC activities recorded in its workload tracking systems and stated that it will incorporate these procedures into its formal policies. Further, the Administration on Aging stated its view that addressing our recommendation to develop written procedures to verify that HCFAC payroll expenditures are reasonable and supported would not provide material results to justify the additional expense and workload. However, the Administration on Aging agreed to explore other options to refine its HCFAC payroll expenditures.

The Office of the General Counsel agreed and stated that it had addressed our recommendation to develop written procedures that incorporate monitoring controls for staff hours recorded in the workload tracking system. It stated that on February 2, 2011, it provided us procedures for properly accounting for HCFAC expenditures. While we received procedures from the

Office of the General Counsel, these procedures did not address our finding. Instead, the procedures discussed the transfer of payroll expenditures to the HCFAC account. Therefore, we determined that this recommendation has not been addressed.

CMS disagreed with our recommendation to revise procedures for maintaining supporting documentation for HCFAC deposits and expenditures, which include specifying the titles of staff responsible for maintaining supporting documentation.

CMS stated that the National Archives and Records Administration does not require staff titles on a standard form it prescribes for transferring records to approved records facilities (SF-135) and that CMS requires staff to take records retention training each year. CMS also stated it believes the information maintained is sufficient to ensure accountability and proper and consistent supporting documentation for HCFAC deposits and expenditures. However, we continue to believe that CMS's policies and procedures for documentation are insufficient, as they do not identify the staff responsible for maintaining documentation as required by the National Archives and Records Administration regulations.[41] Also, CMS stated that the creation of a new records retention system for HCFAC records would be duplicative and unnecessary.

We do not believe that a new records retention system exclusively for HCFAC records is necessary to achieve accountability for documentation responsibilities. Rather, a modification to CMS's existing procedures that identifies the responsible staff by title to show authority levels for properly maintaining supporting documentation, help provide continuity when staff change positions, and promote accountability would be sufficient to address this shortcoming.

Lastly, in its comments, CMS did not address our remaining recommendation to develop written procedures that incorporate monitoring controls for HCFAC deposit information recorded in the departmentwide accounting system.

However, as we stated in the report, CMS officials told us in February 2011 that they were in the process of developing procedures that require the reconciliation of HCFAC deposit information.

Sincerely yours,

Kay L. Daly
Director, Financial Management and Assurance

APPENDIX I: OBJECTIVES, SCOPE, AND METHODOLOGY

The objectives of this review were to determine to what extent the Department of Health and Human Services (HHS) and the Department of Justice (DOJ) (1) took action to address the recommendations we made in 2005 and (2) designed effective controls over reporting Health Care Fraud and Abuse Control (HCFAC) program deposits and expenditures for fiscal years 2008 and 2009.[1]

To address the extent to which HHS and DOJ took action to address the recommendations made in 2005, we:

- Obtained and reviewed documentation provided by HHS and DOJ such as policies and procedures and the *Report Completion Guide*.
- Interviewed officials at HHS and DOJ including the Acting Deputy Inspector General and the Assistant Director of the Executive Office for United States Attorneys to identify actions to improve HCFAC program operations.

To address the extent to which HHS and DOJ designed effective controls over reporting HCFAC deposits and expenditures, we:

- Obtained and reviewed relevant HHS and DOJ policies and procedures for reporting deposits and expenditures within each agency.[2]
- Used criteria outlined in our *Standards for Internal Control in the Federal Government*, specifically as it relates to control activities and monitoring, to assess the effectiveness of controls over the reporting of amounts related to deposits and expenditures. We applied these standards to assess whether the design of the controls documented in the policies and procedures reasonably assured accurate and consistent reporting of HCFAC amounts in the joint annual HCFAC report.3 We did not verify the validity or accuracy of the reported amounts.
- Assessed the reliability of data used to select our nongeneralizable samples by:
    - tracing deposit control totals of the electronic databases to the corresponding deposit line item totals reported in the HCFAC

reports and the Bureau of the Public Debt's Federal Hospital Insurance Trust Fund (HI trust fund) statements;

- obtaining the funding decision memorandum detailing how the HCFAC funds would be distributed between HHS and DOJ for fiscal years 2008 and 2009 to verify the HCFAC funds certified by HHS and DOJ officials;
- comparing amounts reported in the joint HCFAC reports to the approved funding decision memorandum and comparing amounts from the decision memorandum to the Office of Management and Budget (OMB) documentation (Apportionment Schedule SF-132) to verify that the amounts were made available;
- tracing total expenditure amounts to supporting documentation, including electronic databases, billing packages, and intra- and interagency agreements; and
- reviewing existing information about the electronic data and the systems that produced them.

We determined that the data were sufficiently reliable to select our samples.

- Selected a nongeneralizable stratified random sample for each of the deposit types (gifts and bequests, criminal fines, civil monetary penalties, and penalties and multiple damages) that HHS and DOJ reported a dollar amount greater than zero in the fiscal years 2008 and 2009 annual HCFAC reports. We selected a total of 47 deposit transactions for fiscal year 2008 and 55 transactions for fiscal year 2009. Transaction selection criteria included various factors such as dollar amounts and transaction volume. For the selected transactions, we reviewed various sources of documentation depending on the type of deposit to determine whether dollar amounts were accurately reported. Examples of supporting documentation for deposits included check registers; electronic fedwires;4 health care tracking forms used to allocate deposit collections among the various health care programs; judgment orders and agency letters identifying applicable fines and penalties assessed; and collection system query reports. These randomly selected transactions were designed to provide additional details about the processing of those transactions and were not intended to be representative of the universe of HCFAC transactions. See appendix II for information about the universe of transactions and our sampled items.

- Selected a nongeneralizable random sample of expenditures for each of the agency components that were allocated HCFAC appropriation funds as reported in the annual HCFAC reports for fiscal years 2008 and 2009.5 For the Centers for Medicare & Medicaid Services (CMS) and the United States Attorneys Office (USAO), we obtained electronic databases and selected a nongeneralizable stratified random sample for those agency components. We selected a total of 63 transactions for fiscal year 2008 and 62 transactions for fiscal year 2009 related to payroll and nonpayroll expenditures. Transaction selection criteria included various factors such as dollar amounts, transaction volume, and source of information. For these transactions, we reviewed various sources of documentation depending on the type of expenditure to determine whether dollar amounts were accurately reported and the use of funds were consistent with the Health Insurance Portability and Accountability Act of 1996 (HIPAA). Examples of supporting documentation for expenditures included workload tracking system and payroll system query reports; time and attendance reports; salary forms; invoices; contracts; and travel vouchers. These randomly selected transactions were designed to provide additional details about the processing of those transactions and were not intended to be representative of the universe of HCFAC transactions. See appendix II for information about the universe of transactions and our sampled items.
- Performed additional procedures for HHS Office of Inspector General (OIG) payroll transactions as this component received 67 percent and 42 percent of total HCFAC appropriations allocated for fiscal years 2008 and 2009, respectively. Specifically, we (1) obtained time reports from workload tracking systems for all four OIG components (Office of Audit Services, Office of Investigations, Office of Evaluations and Inspections, and Office of Counsel to the Inspector General) to determine if the projects identified as HCFAC were properly classified; and (2) compared the number of hours in the workload tracking systems to the number of hours in the HHS payroll system to determine if the components' systems included hours for all staff.
- Interviewed agency officials from HHS and DOJ including budget analysts and financial specialists to obtain an understanding and

clarification of the processes used to report deposits to the HI trust fund and appropriations from this fund, including related expenditures.

We conducted our work from February 2010 through May 2011 in accordance with U.S. generally accepted government auditing standards. Those standards require that we plan and perform the audit to obtain sufficient, appropriate evidence to provide a reasonable basis for our findings and conclusions based on our audit objectives. We believe that the evidence obtained provides a reasonable basis for our findings and conclusions based on our audit objectives.

Appendix II: Information about the Universe of Transactions and Our Sampled Items

During our review of fiscal years 2008 and 2009 Health Care Fraud and Abuse Control (HCFAC) program activities, we selected nongeneralizable samples to further understand the Department of Health and Human Services (HHS) and the Department of Justice (DOJ) procedures for HCFAC deposits and expenditures. For deposits, we stratified the data and selected random transactions, as summarized in table 1 below, for each of the deposit types authorized by the Health Insurance Portability and Accountability Act of 1996 (HIPAA) for which HHS and DOJ reported dollar amounts greater than zero in the fiscal years 2008 and 2009 HCFAC reports.

Table 1. Summary of Selected Deposit Transactions

Line item	Universe of transactions	Total value of universe	Number of selected transactions	Total value of selected transactions
2008				
Criminal fines	200	$2,307,754	10	$1,650,768
Civil monetary penalties[a]	2,568	13,613,590	23	4,304,620
Penalties and multiple damages[a]	273	559,988,531	11	236,905,878
Gifts and bequests	3	25,847	3	25,847
Total	3,044	$575,935,722	47	$242,887,113
2009				
Criminal fines	201	$620,888,618	11	$620,113,917

Table 1. (Continued)

Line item	Universe of transactions	Total value of universe	Number of selected transactions	Total value of selected transactions
Civil monetary penalties[a]	2,610	18,080,194	25	6,184,843
Penalties and multiple damagesa	260	498,671,480	12	477,294,549
Gifts and bequests	7	46,271	7	46,271
Total	3,078	$1,137,686,563	55	$1,103,639,580

Source: GAO analysis of HHS and DOJ HCFAC data.

[a] Total value of selected transactions for civil monetary penalties and penalties and multiple damages represent the absolute value for these line items.

For expenditures, we selected samples from object classes that in aggregate accounted for 50 percent or more of total obligations for each component that received HCFAC funds. Based on dollar amounts, we then selected random transactions, as summarized in table 2 below.

Table 2. Summary of Selected Expenditures Transactions

Agency Component	Number of selected transactions	Value of selected transactions	Object classes selected
2008			
Department of Health and Human Services			
Office of Inspector General	5	$8,570,351	Other Contractual Services. Analytical procedures performed for personnel payroll hours, as described in appendix I.
Office of the General Counsel	4	855,515	Personnel Compensation and Other Contractual Services
Administration on Aging	1	909,997	Grants, Subsidies, and Contributions
Centers for Medicare & Medicaid Services	14	11,906,880	Personnel Compensation and Other Contractual Services
Department of Justice			
United States Attorneys Office	7	3,635,898	Personnel Compensation and Rent, Communications, and Utilities
Civil Divisiona	12	5,271,253	Personnel Compensation and Other Contractual Services
Criminal Division	10	427,156	Personnel Compensation; Rent,

Agency Component	Number of selected transactions	Value of selected transactions	Object classes selected
			Communications, and Utilities; and Other Contractual Services
Civil Rights	10	79,423	Personnel Compensation and OtherContractual Services
Total 2008	63	$31,656,473	
2009			
Department of Health and Human Services			
Office of Inspector General	5	2,584,748	Other Contractual Services. Analytical procedures performed for personnel payroll hours, as described in appendix I.
Office of the General Counsel	1	6,695	Personnel Compensation
Administration on Aging	1	646,773	Grants, Subsidies, and Contributions
Centers for Medicare & Medicaid Services	18	72,241,840	Personnel Compensation and OtherContractual Services
Department of Justice			
United States Attorneys Office	7	3,642,137	Personnel Compensation and Rent,Communications, and Utilities
Civil Divisiona	10	2,496,884	Personnel Compensation and OtherContractual Services
Criminal Division	11	478,988	Personnel Compensation; Rent, Communications, and Utilities; Other Contractual Services; and Supplies and Materials
Civil Rights	9	61,320	Personnel Compensation and Other Contractual Services
Total 2009	62	$82,159,385	

Source: GAO analysis of HHS and DOJ HCFAC data.

[a] Samples selected for Civil Division also include transactions for the Nursing Home and Elderly Justice Initiative.

End Notes

[1] GAO, High-Risk Series: An Update, GAO-11-278 (Washington, D.C.: February 2011). Fraud represents intentional acts of deception with knowledge that the action or representation could result in an inappropriate gain. Waste includes inaccurate payments for services, such as unintentional duplicate payments. Abuse represents actions inconsistent with acceptable

business or medical practices. An improper payment is defined as any payment that should not have been made or that was made in an incorrect amount (including overpayments and underpayments) under statutory, contractual, administrative, or other legally applicable requirements. It includes any payment to an ineligible recipient, any payment for an ineligible service, any duplicate payment, any payment for services not received, and any payment that does not account for credit for applicable discounts. The Office of Management and Budget (OMB) guidance also instructs agencies to report payments for which insufficient or no documentation was found as improper payments.

[2] For fiscal year 2010, HHS reported improper payment estimates for the following programs: $34.3 billion for Medicare Fee-for-Service (FFS); $13.6 million for Medicare Advantage; and $22.5 billion (the estimated federal share) for Medicaid.

[3] See appendix III of GAO's audit report included in the fiscal year 2010 Financial Report of the United States Government accessible at http://www.fms.treas.gov/fr/index.html.

[4] Pub. L. No. 104-191, § 201, 110 Stat. 1936, 1992 (Aug. 21, 1996).

[5] The HI trust fund was established on July 30, 1965, as a separate account in the U.S. Department of the Treasury. It is also known as the Medicare Trust Fund. The HI trust fund finances the Medicare Part A program, which helps pay for hospital, home health, skilled nursing facility, and hospice care for the aged and disabled. All of the HI financial operations are handled through this fund, including the revenues and expenditures related to the HCFAC program as authorized by HIPAA and other funding streams such as payroll taxes transferred to the HI trust fund and net benefit payments.

[6] GAO, Health Care Fraud and Abuse Control Program: Results of Review of Annual Reports for Fiscal Years 2002 and 2003, GAO-05-134 (Washington, D.C.: Apr. 29, 2005).

[7] HHS and DOJ, The Department of Health and Human Services and the Department of Justice Health Care Fraud and Abuse Control Program Annual Report For FY 2008 (Washington, D.C.: September 2009); and The Department of Health and Human Services and the Department of Justice Health Care Fraud and Abuse Control Program Annual Report For FY 2009 (Washington, D.C.: May 2010).

[8] GAO, Internal Control: Standards for Internal Control in the Federal Government, GAO/AIMD-00-21.3.1 (Washington, D.C.: November 1999).

[9] See 18 U.S.C. §§ 24(a), 1341.

[10] There are 94 offices throughout the United States, Puerto Rico, the Virgin Islands, Guam, and the Northern Mariana Islands.

[11] The United States District Courts, which operate under the Judicial Branch, and DOJ's United States Attorneys Office (USAO), which operate under the Executive Branch, have different responsibilities for the management of criminal debt. The collection and management of criminal debt require the cooperation of both branches of government. USAOs are statutorily responsible for the enforcement of the collection of criminal debt, while the District Courts receive payments of fines.

[12] The Executive Office for the United States Attorneys provides general executive assistance and supervision to the USAOs, among other functions.

[13] See, e.g., 42 U.S.C. §§ 1320a-7a, 1395i-3, & 1396r(h). 1418 U.S.C. § 982(a)(7).

[15] We did not independently assess whether the reported zero deposit amounts for asset forfeiture in the annual HCFAC reports for fiscal years 2008 and 2009 were accurate.

[16] These suits can also be brought by private individuals, called relators, under the False Claims Act, 31 U.S.C. §§ 3729-33. Relators can be entitled to a portion of any court award or settlement, and this relator's share is not included in the amount credited to the HI trust fund.

[17] Pub. L. No. 107-273, § 11013, 116 Stat. 1758, 1823 (Nov. 2, 2002).

[18] Medicare Parts A and B are also known as Medicare fee-for-service (FFS). Medicare Part A covers hospital and other inpatient stays and Medicare Part B covers hospital outpatient, physician, and other services. The Federal Supplementary Medical Insurance (SMI) Trust Fund finances the Medicare Part B program.

[19] In general, restitutions restore the aggrieved party to its prior state of well-being while compensatory damages reimburse the aggrieved party for losses incurred.

[20] Collections such as these that represent a refund of erroneous expenditures are credited back to the appropriation that was originally charged for those expenditures. See, e.g., B281064 (Feb. 14, 2000).

[21] HHS and DOJ may also conduct other health care fraud enforcement activities using other annual appropriations.

[22] An allotment is an authorization by either the agency head or another authorized employee to his/her subordinates to incur obligations within a specified amount. Each agency makes allotments pursuant to specific procedures it establishes in accordance with the Office of Management and Budget (OMB) general apportionment requirements. See OMB Circular No. A-11, Preparation, Submission, and Execution of the Budget, Part 4 (November 2010).

[23] The IPAC System's primary purpose is to provide a standardized interagency fund transfer mechanism for federal agencies. IPAC facilitates the intra-governmental transfer of funds, with descriptive data from one federal agency to another.

[24] Mandatory funding refers to budgetary resources that are controlled by laws other than appropriations acts.

[25] Discretionary funding refers to budgetary resources that are provided in annual appropriation acts, other than those that fund mandatory programs. Discretionary funds appropriated to the HCFAC account were transferred from the HI and SMI trust funds. Omnibus Appropriations Act, 2009, Pub. L. No. 111-8, 123 Stat. 524, 773 (Mar. 11, 2009).

[26] Pub. L. No. 109-432, div. b, § 303, 120 Stat. 2922, 2992 (Dec. 20, 2006). In fiscal year 2010, the Patient Protection and Affordable Care Act extended permanently the yearly increases to the HCFAC account based on the change in the CPI-U.

[27] Pub. L. No. 111-148, § 6402(i), 124 Stat. 119, 760 (Mar. 23, 2010).

[28] Pub. L. No. 111-152, § 1303(a), 124 Stat. 1029, 1057 (Mar. 30, 2010).

[29] GAO-05-134.

[30] In our 2005 report, we made a total of three recommendations. One of the three recommendations included two parts, which for purposes of this report, we identify as two separate recommendations, making a total of four.

[31] The sample selections were not designed to be representative of the universe of HCFAC transactions, but rather to provide anecdotal information. For this purpose, we selected a total nongeneralizable sample of 102 HCFAC deposits for fiscal years 2008 and 2009 and a total nongeneralizable sample of 125 HCFAC expenditures for fiscal years 2008 and 2009. For additional information about our sampling methodology, see appendix II.

[32] Policies and procedures reviewed for HHS included OIG and the Office of the General Counsel records management plans, and the Administration on Aging's retention policy for the Office of Budget and Finance. CMS policies and procedures reviewed included: CMS Records Schedule, General Records Schedule 6: Accountable Officers' Accounts Records, and policies for purging files issued by the Office of Strategic Operations and Regulatory Affairs.

[33] DOJ policies and procedures reviewed included: USAP 3-11.310.001 Internal Controls for Processing Payments Received for Civil Debts and Criminal Impositions—Retention of

Records and Financial Management Policies and Procedures Bulletin 00-15 Accounting for Financial Obligations Within the Offices, Boards and Divisions (OBDs).

[34] GAO/AIMD-00-21.3.1.

[35] HHS and DOJ transmit HCFAC collection information to the Bureau of the Public Debt, which has responsibility for administering the HI trust fund. The Bureau of the Public Debt transfers from the Treasury General Fund to the HI trust fund an amount equal to the sum of fines, penalties, and other designated monies collected from health care investigations.

[36] The Office of Financial Management utilizes the ASPEN Enforcement Manager (AEM) and Financial Accounting Control System (FACS) to allocate and record payments received. AEM enables CMS regional offices to manage all tasks related to nursing home enforcement. FACS accumulates all of CMS's financial activities, both programmatic and administrative, in its general ledger.

[37] Debt Collection Management Staff within the Justice Management Division is responsible for establishing policies related to federal debt collection efforts, operating the department's central intake facility for civil debt collections, and performing debt accounting operations.

[38] DOJ collects payments for penalties and multiple damages from debtors and uses its financial system to record these collections. DOJ is entitled to keep 3 percent of all payments collected in its Working Capital Fund for paying the costs of processing and tracking civil and criminal debt collection litigations.

[39] HIPAA does not specify how costs are to be charged against the HCFAC account. HHS and DOJ components use different processes for charging payroll costs against HCFAC funds. For example, some components within HHS and DOJ charged 100 percent of staff hours to HCFAC while others charged a percentage of total staff hours based on estimated or actual performance. To accomplish this, HHS and DOJ components calculated estimates based on prior year performance or used their workload tracking systems to monitor actual hours spent on HCFAC activities.

[40] GAO/AIMD-00-21.3.1.

[41] The National Archives and Records Administration regulations require each agency to develop internal policies and procedures to ensure proper maintenance of records. These regulations also indicate that agency programs must develop recordkeeping requirements that include identification of the location of the records and the staff responsible for maintaining the records. See 36 C.F.R. § 1220.34 and subpart 1222.B.

End Notes for Appendix I

[1] GAO-05-134.

[2] HHS policies and procedures obtained and reviewed included the Office of Investigations Policies and Procedures Manual; collection procedures for civil monetary penalties; and policies for records management. DOJ policies and procedures obtained and reviewed included Financial Management Policies and Procedures Bulletins 08-02, 08-01, 05-15 and 00-15, and United States Attorneys Office Procedures 3-11.120.001, 3-11.120.002, and 3-11.310.001. For both agencies, we also obtained and reviewed the different information system user manuals such as accounting systems, collection systems, and workload tracking systems.

[3] GAO/AIMD-00-21.3.1.

[4] Fedwire is the Federal Reserve's real-time gross settlement system that enables participants to initiate large-value funds transfer that are immediate, final, and irrevocable once processed.

[5] HHS components included the Office of Inspector General (OIG), Centers for Medicare & Medicaid Services (CMS), Office of the General Counsel, and Administration on Aging. DOJ components included United States Attorneys Office (USAO), Civil Division, Criminal Division, and Civil Rights Division.

INDEX

#

21st century, 99

A

abuse, vii, 1, 2, 3, 4, 5, 8, 9, 11, 31, 45, 62, 63, 64, 65, 66, 68, 69, 71, 74, 81, 83, 84, 85, 86, 88, 89, 93, 94, 97, 102, 103, 104, 109, 118, 120, 122, 125, 126, 127
access, 14, 58, 60, 67
accountability, 130, 139
accounting, 62, 119, 123, 124, 125, 127, 128, 132, 133, 136, 137, 138, 139, 148
accreditation, 69
activity level, 133
AD, 34
ADA, 104, 107, 108
adjunctive therapy, 24
adjustment, 51, 78, 88, 114
administrative support, 9
adults, 24, 41, 83
adverse event, 54
advertisements, 73
age, 24, 28, 50, 61, 92
agencies, 2, 5, 13, 26, 41, 50, 51, 52, 80, 86, 87, 88, 96, 100, 101, 102, 109, 110, 111, 119, 120, 123, 127, 129, 132, 146, 147, 148
allergy, 92
American Recovery and Reinvestment Act, 115
American Recovery and Reinvestment Act of 2009, 115
Americans with Disabilities Act, 104
antipsychotic, 60
antipsychotic drugs, 60
anxiety, 25
APA, 89
appropriations, 4, 114, 123, 125, 142, 143, 147
Appropriations Act, 5, 115, 126
Armenia, 103
arrest, 100
arrests, 71, 82, 101
arthritis, 17
assessment, 55, 71
assets, 25, 88
Attorney General, vii, 1, 3, 4, 7, 8, 9, 44, 92, 99, 122, 125, 126, 128, 129, 137
audit(s), 3, 4, 6, 8, 14, 45, 48, 50, 52, 53, 54, 55, 56, 62, 64, 70, 71, 72, 75, 78, 88, 114, 122, 125, 127, 135, 143, 146
authority(s), 47, 61, 65, 87, 90, 98, 104, 139
automation, 75
automobiles, 23
average costs, 77

avoidance, 67
awareness, 9, 83, 92

B

bankruptcy, 90
base, 52
beneficiaries, vii, 2, 9, 10, 13, 14, 15, 16, 17, 18, 19, 20, 21, 22, 23, 29, 32, 35, 41, 42, 44, 45, 48, 50, 51, 54, 57, 58, 59, 61, 62, 64, 68, 70, 72, 73, 76, 77, 81, 82, 83, 84, 93, 120
benefits, 21, 32, 43, 85
benign, 30
bipolar disorder, 60
blood, 12, 25, 26, 55, 102
blood clot, 26
bonds, 59, 69
bone, 26
brain, 31, 107
breakdown, 4, 5
bribes, 13
browser, 67
budgetary resources, 147
businesses, 23, 30, 98

C

CAP, 74
caregivers, 58
cash, 15, 16, 23, 37
casinos, 23
catastrophes, 17
Centers for Medicare & Medicaid Services (CMS), 2, 5, 123, 124, 142, 149
certificate, 47
certification, 3, 76
CFR, 63, 69
challenges, 86
chemical, 18
Chicago, 10, 11, 22, 23, 111, 115
children, 34, 41
cholesterol, 101
chronic illness, 99
CIA, 25, 28, 33, 37, 39, 40, 42, 43, 64, 112
city(s), 10, 11, 27, 42, 63, 69, 92, 100, 101, 111
civil action, 104
civil monetary penalties, 3, 47, 124, 134, 141, 144, 148
civil settlements, 3, 94
classes, 68, 101, 144
clients, 37
clinical diagnosis, 78
clinical trials, 26
clustering, 68
coding, 29
collaboration, 8, 75, 77, 78, 137, 138
commerce, 23, 25, 98
common law, 29
communication, 72, 91
community(s), 9, 14, 18, 48, 63, 83, 84, 95, 106, 107, 108
community service, 108
community support, 106, 107
community-based services, 107, 108
competitors, 35
compilation, 134
complement, 91
complexity, 120
compliance, 9, 39, 50, 52, 54, 56, 63, 64, 70, 72, 74, 77, 85, 87, 88, 97, 106, 109, 114
complications, 31
compression, 26
compression fracture, 26
conduction, 16
conference, 10, 82, 93, 102
confidentiality, 102
confinement, 18, 104
Congress, vii, 4, 7, 11, 15, 44, 64, 75, 76, 88, 114, 118, 119, 120, 123, 125, 126, 127, 129, 135, 136
consent, 35, 43, 47
conspiracy, 16, 17, 21, 22, 25, 26, 30, 39, 40, 44, 46, 91, 99, 101
Constitution, 104

consulting, 29, 38, 52
consumer price index, 4, 113, 117, 126
consumers, 4, 69, 71, 83, 117, 126
contamination, 24
controlled substances, 20, 30, 46, 99
Controlled Substances Act, 62
conviction, 12, 17, 30, 33, 46, 58
cooperation, 101, 146
coordination, 9, 91, 103
corruption, 102
cost, 27, 29, 31, 35, 38, 51, 52, 56, 62, 67, 77, 93, 120, 133, 134
cost saving, 93
counsel, 88
counseling, 29, 83, 84
covering, 72
CPB, 98, 99
CPI, 4, 113, 114, 117, 126, 147
crimes, 2, 26, 45, 58, 94, 110
criminal activity, 110
criminal fines, 3, 26, 124, 141
criminal investigations, 2, 91
criminals, 11
criticism, 76
CT, 107
cures, 98
customers, 24
cycles, 76

D

damages, 3, 6, 90, 111, 120, 124, 125, 132, 134, 137, 141, 144, 147, 148
data analysis, 11, 63, 66, 67, 71, 79, 95
data collection, 124, 132, 136
data mining, 63
data set, 67
database, 66, 68, 70, 75, 122
DEA, 62, 109, 113
deaths, 26, 31, 54
debtors, 90, 148
decision makers, 136
defendants, 2, 10, 11, 12, 13, 15, 16, 18, 19, 20, 21, 22, 24, 26, 34, 42, 91, 95, 99, 100, 101, 110
deficiencies, 72, 74, 130
denial, 87, 90
Department of Health and Human Services, v, vii, 1, 7, 44, 112, 113, 117, 120, 140, 143, 144, 145, 146
Department of Justice, v, 1, 2, 7, 93, 96, 113, 117, 120, 140, 143, 144, 145, 146
Department of Labor, 103
Department of the Treasury, 2, 5
deposits, viii, 5, 111, 118, 119, 121, 122, 124, 129, 130, 132, 136, 137, 139, 140, 141, 143, 147
dermatologist, 30
detection, 81, 91, 102
detention, 15
detoxification, 27
diabetic patients, 35
dialysis, 34, 44
directives, 131
directors, 28
disability, 47
disclosure, 85, 102
discrimination, 104
dismantlement, 2, 109, 110
distribution, 23, 46, 96
District of Columbia, 45, 51, 105
DME, 11, 13, 14, 15, 17, 18, 19, 20, 22, 35, 36, 48, 59, 60, 68, 81, 87, 90, 113
doctors, 10, 18, 19, 25, 35, 37, 43, 97, 99, 100, 101
domestic markets, 73
Dominican Republic, 16
donations, 124
draft, 89, 102, 138
drug abuse, 99
drug abusers, 99
Drug Enforcement Administration (DEA), 20, 113
drug testing, 37
drug treatment, 99
drugs, 15, 20, 23, 25, 31, 33, 46, 53, 60, 61, 62, 86, 91, 94, 96, 98, 99, 101

E

education, 50, 55, 56, 59, 70, 78, 81, 83, 84, 90, 101
e-mail, 138
emergency, 43, 46, 47, 48
employees, 9, 20, 23, 35, 36, 40, 41, 58, 92, 128
employers, 102
employment, 36, 47, 58, 102, 103
end stage renal disease (ESRD), 34
endometriosis, 29
enforcement, 4, 8, 9, 47, 68, 72, 81, 82, 85, 87, 88, 89, 94, 97, 100, 101, 102, 104, 108, 122, 125, 146, 147, 148
enrollment, 56, 65, 67, 69, 80, 85, 87
epidemic, 99
epilepsy, 24, 25
equipment, 17, 18, 22, 34, 59, 69, 82, 99, 111
ESRD, 34
evidence, 13, 14, 15, 17, 19, 25, 30, 55, 79, 87, 122, 143
evidence-based practices, 55
examinations, 92
exclusion, 32, 45, 47, 50, 64
Executive Order, 77
expenditures, viii, 53, 61, 84, 109, 118, 119, 121, 123, 125, 127, 128, 129, 130, 131, 132, 133, 134, 136, 137, 138, 139, 140, 142, 143, 144, 146, 147
expertise, 63, 99
exploitation, 97

F

family members, 21
family planning, 50
FBI, 4, 10, 11, 44, 58, 82, 88, 100, 102, 108, 109, 110, 111, 113, 114
FDA, 24, 25, 26, 31, 32, 38, 60, 62, 90, 91, 92, 98, 99, 102, 109, 110, 113
federal agency, 147
Federal Bureau of Investigation (FBI), 2, 7, 108, 113
federal funds, 49
federal government, 120, 121, 129, 131, 135, 140, 146
federal regulations, 34, 49, 61
ferret, 71
financial, 37, 39, 45, 49, 52, 62, 69, 74, 75, 89, 97, 122, 127, 142, 146, 148
financial oversight, 74
financial reports, 49
financial system, 148
fiscal year 2009, 120, 121, 125, 128, 131, 132, 133, 134, 141, 142
flexibility, 63
Food and Drug Administration, 7, 24, 90, 113
force, 46, 127
forfeitures, 3, 94, 98, 124
formal education, 43
fractures, 27
funding, 4, 7, 9, 11, 44, 53, 63, 64, 70, 74, 82, 83, 85, 90, 92, 93, 96, 97, 99, 103, 108, 111, 112, 114, 115, 122, 125, 126, 127, 134, 141, 146, 147
funds, 3, 5, 6, 8, 23, 27, 41, 44, 45, 48, 53, 54, 63, 64, 71, 79, 85, 86, 88, 90, 92, 94, 95, 112, 114, 120, 121, 122, 125, 126, 127, 128, 131, 135, 141, 142, 144, 147, 148, 149
future fraud, vii, 2

G

gambling, 23
GAO, viii, 117, 118, 119, 123, 127, 129, 131, 135, 144, 145, 146, 147, 148
Georgia, 27, 42, 105, 107, 108
glucose, 55
goods and services, 25, 102
government funds, 40
grants, 25, 102
greed, 47

guidance, 4, 54, 59, 62, 64, 78, 97, 99, 100, 102, 103, 111, 122, 128, 135, 146
guidelines, 26, 34, 55
guilty, 11, 12, 14, 16, 17, 18, 19, 21, 22, 23, 24, 25, 30, 32, 35, 39, 40, 71, 98, 100

H

headache, 25
Health and Human Services, vii, 8, 118, 146
health care costs, 9, 91
Health Care Fraud and Abuse Control Program (HCFAC), vii
Health Care Fraud Prevention & Enforcement Action Team (HEAT), 8
health care programs, vii, 2, 5, 8, 24, 26, 27, 32, 33, 37, 40, 43, 45, 47, 64, 96, 100, 111, 118, 120, 122, 127, 141
health care sector, 65
health care system, 94, 109, 110
health insurance, 103
health services, 12, 14, 40, 52
health status, 77
hemophilia, 25
hemorrhage, 25
Hispanic population, 83
historical data, 66
history, 58, 88
HIV, 11, 12, 13, 15, 16, 30, 113
homes, 50, 58, 97, 104, 107, 108
hospice, 33, 58, 146
host, 82
hot spots, 11, 95
hotels, 30
hotspots, 86
human, 26, 47
human resources, 47
husband, 22

I

ID, 68
identification, 75, 78, 103, 148
identity, 14, 21, 82
imprisonment, 12, 26, 31
improvements, 45
incarceration, 11, 16, 17, 32, 35, 40, 44, 46, 47
incidence, 54, 92
income, 14, 54, 72, 76, 78, 120
individuals, 2, 17, 19, 26, 30, 33, 40, 45, 50, 51, 68, 71, 82, 98, 100, 102, 103, 104, 107, 108, 111, 124, 146
industry, 4, 35, 66, 78, 87, 103, 111, 122
information sharing, 9
infrastructure, 83
ingredients, 53
initiation, 104
injections, 29, 48
injury(s), 12, 46, 107
inspections, 4, 127, 134
institutions, 104, 107, 108
insulin, 13, 55
integration, 66, 67, 108
integrity, 64, 65, 68, 70, 71, 72, 79, 83, 84, 85, 86, 88, 89, 90, 125
intelligence, 9, 11, 82
interagency coordination, 99
interface, 67
interferon, 37
internal controls, 49, 62
Internal Revenue Service, 44, 109
intervention, 54
investment, 8, 54
Israel, 48
issues, 9, 10, 74, 80, 83, 84, 86, 87, 88, 89, 91, 92, 95, 97, 102, 108, 111, 130

J

Jordan, 106
Judicial Branch, 146
jurisdiction, 109

justification, 4, 121, 131

L

labeling, 98
law enforcement, vii, 1, 4, 8, 9, 10, 15, 67, 68, 70, 71, 79, 80, 81, 82, 84, 85, 88, 92, 94, 96, 97, 99, 100, 102, 110, 112, 122, 127
laws, 8, 64, 103, 127, 147
laws and regulations, 103
lead, 21, 67, 73, 78, 133
leadership, 8, 99, 100
legal issues, 86
legislation, 54, 123
legislative proposals, 45, 102, 103
lesions, 30
light, 84
lipids, 25, 102
litigation, 85, 86, 88, 89, 90, 93, 99, 100, 101, 102, 103, 108, 127
lobbying, 15
local government, 108
Louisiana, 19, 43, 101, 108
LTC, 47

M

macular degeneration, 61
mail fraud, 35, 91, 123
majority, 20, 76, 109
man, 23, 35
management, 23, 25, 36, 42, 75, 100, 102, 115, 129, 131, 135, 146, 147, 148
Mandarin, 73
manipulation, 86
manslaughter, 46
manufacturing, 23, 91, 94, 96, 98
marketing, 24, 25, 26, 37, 38, 39, 42, 72, 73, 74, 86, 91, 94
marketplace, 72
Maryland, 33
materials, 63, 70, 83, 97, 99, 102
matter, 32, 35, 37, 40, 74, 86, 97, 101, 115
measurement, 64, 76, 77, 79
media, 70, 83, 93
medical, 12, 13, 15, 16, 17, 18, 19, 21, 23, 25, 28, 29, 30, 34, 36, 37, 38, 42, 44, 46, 47, 48, 51, 54, 55, 59, 61, 62, 64, 69, 77, 78, 81, 90, 91, 94, 95, 97, 99, 101, 102, 104, 110, 124, 146
medical goods, 37, 97
medication, 23
medicine, 18, 41
mental health, 12, 49, 104, 107
mental illness, 104, 105, 106, 107, 108
methadone, 62
methodology, 51, 68, 70, 77, 122, 147
Miami, 11, 12, 13, 15, 21, 56, 69, 79, 81, 92, 93, 100, 111
microorganisms, 24
microscope, 99
military, 25, 44
MIP, 64, 77, 112, 114
mission, 8, 9, 91
Missouri, 30, 69, 98, 108
misuse, 31
models, 66
modifications, 89
modules, 63
money laundering, 15, 16, 40, 44, 46
mood disorder, 25
moratorium, 56, 65
morphine, 98
MR, 42
multiple sclerosis, 37

N

narcotic(s), 15, 46
neglect, 2, 45, 94, 97, 104
negotiation, 97
nerve, 16, 31
neurologist, 18
nurses, 10, 100, 101

nursing, 13, 32, 33, 36, 41, 51, 52, 57, 58, 90, 94, 97, 103, 104, 105, 107, 108, 146, 148
nursing care, 41
nursing home, 33, 36, 58, 90, 94, 97, 103, 104, 107, 148
nutrients, 20

O

occupational therapy, 15, 16, 21, 36
offenders, 109
Office of Justice Programs, 98
Office of Management and Budget, 118, 141, 146, 147
Office of the Inspector General, 113
officials, viii, 16, 40, 50, 79, 93, 118, 119, 121, 128, 129, 132, 133, 134, 135, 139, 140, 141, 142
OH, 39
Oklahoma, 28, 50
OMB, 118, 141, 146, 147
omission, 91
Omnibus Appropriations Act,, 147
operations, 3, 10, 24, 100, 109, 110, 111, 135, 140, 146, 148
opportunities, 73
orthopedic surgeon, 38, 47
outpatient, 15, 27, 28, 37, 49, 53, 55, 56, 127, 147
outreach, 39, 70, 72, 78, 81, 83, 84, 93
oversight, 9, 28, 52, 55, 63, 71, 72, 89, 100, 114, 115, 120, 129
ownership, 28

P

pain, 25, 48, 98
parallel, 101
partial seizure, 24
participants, 63, 93, 149
Paxil, 23
payroll, 119, 121, 125, 127, 131, 133, 134, 137, 138, 139, 142, 144, 145, 146, 148
PCT, 63
penalties, 3, 6, 26, 41, 47, 98, 124, 132, 134, 137, 141, 144, 148
permission, 21
permit, 50, 64, 67
perpetrators, 9
persons with disabilities, 104
pharmaceutical, 9, 24, 86, 91, 94, 95, 96, 97, 98
Philadelphia, 10, 79, 92
Philippines, 23
physical therapist, 19, 21
physical therapy, 16, 19, 21, 41
physicians, 15, 20, 23, 25, 31, 34, 35, 37, 38, 39, 42, 43, 46, 49, 55, 62, 70, 78, 82, 87, 94, 96, 97, 101
policy, 45, 55, 75, 79, 102, 127, 147
population, 83
prejudice, 107
preparation, 50, 135
prescription drugs, 32, 33, 38, 73, 99
president, 15, 21, 31, 77, 79, 123
President Obama, 79
prevention, 9, 10, 60, 64, 65, 79, 81, 87, 93
price index, 4
private sector, 9, 10, 66, 79, 102, 103, 111
professionals, 25, 29, 63, 83, 101
profit, 23, 37, 58
program beneficiaries, vii, 2, 45
program staff, 84
programming, 66
project, 66, 70, 71, 74, 79, 80, 81, 82, 83, 92
prostate cancer, 29
psychotherapy, 15, 29
public awareness, 70, 92, 93
public health, 91, 99
public sector, 9
publishing, 59, 76
Puerto Rico, 23, 32, 105, 110, 146

pumps, 35

Q

qualifications, 50
quality control, 28
query, 141, 142
questionnaire, 99
qui tam provisions, 6

R

radiation, 30, 97
radiation treatment, 30
radio, 93
rape, 47
real estate, 23
reality, 21
recall, 26
recognition, 101
recommendations, viii, 3, 45, 51, 55, 59, 61, 92, 118, 119, 121, 127, 136, 138, 140, 147
reconciliation, 77, 132, 134, 136, 137, 139
reconstruction, 38, 39
recovery, 78, 85, 86, 89, 135
recruiting, 15
reforms, 39, 40
regulations, 28, 34, 36, 41, 42, 54, 60, 61, 63, 87, 97, 139, 148
rehabilitation, 36, 48
reimburse, 24, 147
relators, 38, 146
relevance, 129
reliability, 140
relief, 98, 103, 104
remission, 88
requirements, 5, 35, 43, 49, 50, 52, 53, 54, 55, 60, 62, 67, 72, 76, 77, 85, 88, 146, 147, 148
Residential, 105
resolution, 25, 35, 39, 51, 94, 110
resource utilization, 57
resources, 8, 10, 11, 79, 85, 89, 92, 93, 94, 96, 98, 109, 122, 134
response, 76, 81, 93, 107, 110, 125
restitution, 3, 6, 33, 46, 98, 100, 111, 120, 125, 134
restrictions, 62
retail, 24, 73
revenue, 35, 54
RICO, 103
rights, 90, 104, 105, 108
risk, 12, 31, 41, 55, 65, 66, 71, 75, 77, 78, 79, 80, 82, 88, 91, 97, 107, 108, 120, 131, 134, 135
risk assessment, 71
ROI, 8, 70, 111, 112
root, 59
rules, 34, 36, 64, 71, 72, 77, 86, 87, 89, 97
Russia, 103

S

safety, 26, 55, 61, 99, 104
SAS, 66
savings, 45, 54, 67, 80, 82, 84, 85, 89
schizophrenia, 60
school, 51
scope, 43, 64, 71, 81, 96, 122
Secret Service, 88
seminars, 95
Senate, 117, 120
sentencing, 14, 16, 17, 30
service provider, 41, 52, 67
settlements, 3, 7, 27, 45, 85, 94, 97, 114
sexual abuse, 47
sham, 34, 82
shelf life, 61
skin, 30, 32
skin diseases, 30
Social Security, 3, 47, 111, 114, 124
software, 66
specialists, 74, 122, 142
speech, 21, 36
spending, 56, 58, 112, 120
spinal cord, 31

spine, 26
staffing, 47, 98, 100
stakeholders, 70, 72, 76
statistics, 114
statutes, 85, 90, 122
stress, 93
structure, 58
structuring, 107
subscribers, 23
subsidy(s), 72, 78, 144, 145
sulfate, 98
supervision, 20, 39, 40, 41, 52, 146
supplier(s), 3, 4, 11, 18, 22, 35, 44, 45, 47, 59, 60, 65, 67, 68, 69, 70, 80, 82, 85, 86, 87, 88, 90, 97
support services, 34, 39
Supreme Court, 104, 108
surgical intervention, 48
surveillance, 71, 72, 73, 74
susceptibility, 120
suspensions, 59, 86, 87
symptoms, 15, 92

T

tactics, 70, 73
target, 11, 57, 63, 77, 110
Task Force, 99
taxes, 146
teams, 8, 9, 10, 11, 12, 63, 95, 100
technical assistance, 71, 83, 108
technical comments, 138
technician, 46
techniques, 11, 71, 90, 111
technology(s), 9, 63, 64, 66, 67
terminally ill, 33
terminals, 70
testing, 30, 38, 56, 68, 87
theft, 21, 40, 82
therapist, 19, 21, 36
therapy, 11, 15, 16, 19, 21, 25, 28, 34, 35, 36, 41, 52, 56, 57, 80, 81, 102
threats, 109, 110
time frame, 128, 134
tissue, 19
Title I, 104
Title II, 104
trafficking, 21, 30
training, 9, 10, 23, 37, 51, 63, 67, 68, 73, 84, 92, 95, 97, 100, 102, 103, 111, 139
transactions, 64, 121, 131, 141, 142, 143, 144, 145, 147
transparency, 85
transport, 42, 44
transportation, 43, 44
trauma, 25, 46
Treasury, 2, 6, 8, 77, 111, 114, 148
treatment, 20, 22, 24, 46, 60, 61, 92, 99, 101
trial, 12, 13, 14, 15, 16, 17, 18, 19, 22, 30, 91, 92, 94, 95, 100
trust fund, viii, 2, 3, 4, 5, 6, 8, 54, 66, 87, 89, 94, 111, 113, 114, 118, 119, 120, 121, 123, 124, 125, 126, 132, 134, 135, 137, 141, 143, 146, 147, 148

U

U.S. Department of Labor, 18
U.S. Department of the Treasury, 146
unions, 102
universe, 49, 121, 141, 142, 143, 144, 147
updating, 62
urban, 4, 117, 126
USA, 41

V

validation, 78, 88
vehicles, 38
venography, 47
vision, 61
vouchers, 142
vulnerability, 8

W

waiver, 50, 51
Washington, 50, 51, 63, 107, 108, 145, 146
waste, 5, 8, 9, 63, 64, 65, 66, 71, 74, 81, 84, 85, 86, 88, 94, 120
weakness, 130
websites, 31, 73, 99
welfare, 103
well-being, 147
Wisconsin, 42
witnesses, 31, 82, 83, 86
workflow, 75
workforce, 36
working groups, 10, 109
workload, 119, 122, 127, 131, 133, 137, 138, 142, 148